LEADING for DIFFERENTIATION

LEADING for DIFFERENTIATION

Growing Teachers Who Grow Kids

Carol Ann Tomlinson

Michael Murphy

ASCD | Alexandria, VA USA

1703 N. Beauregard St. • Alexandria, VA 22311–1714 USA
Phone: 800-933-2723 or 703-578-9600 • Fax: 703-575-5400
Website: www.ascd.org • E-mail: member@ascd.org
Author guidelines: www.ascd.org/write

Deborah S. Delisle, *Executive Director;* Stefani Roth, *Publisher;* Genny Ostertag, *Director, Content Acquisitions;* Julie Houtz, *Director, Book Editing & Production;* Katie Martin, *Editor;* Donald Ely, *Senior Graphic Designer;* Mike Kalyan, *Manager, Production Services;* Valerie Younkin, *Production Designer;* Andrea Wilson, *Senior Production Specialist*

All web links in this book are correct as of the publication date below but may have become inactive or otherwise modified since that time. If you notice a deactivated or changed link, please e-mail books@ascd.org with the words "Link Update" in the subject line. In your message, please specify the link, the book title, and the page number on which the link appears.

Find downloads associated with this book at www.ascd.org/ASCD/pdf/books/LeadingFor Differentiation.pdf. Enter the password *115005.*

PAPERBACK ISBN: 978-1-4166-2080-8   ASCD product #115005   n9/15

PDF E-BOOK ISBN: 978-1-4166-2082-2; see Books in Print for other formats.

Quantity discounts: 10–49, 10%; 50+, 15%; 1,000+, special discounts (e-mail programteam@ ascd.org or call 800-933-2723, ext. 5773, or 703-575-5773). For desk copies, go to www.ascd. org/deskcopy.

Library of Congress Cataloging-in-Publication Data
Tomlinson, Carol A.
  Leading for differentiation : growing teachers who grow kids / Carol Ann Tomlinson & Michael Murphy.
    pages cm
  Includes bibliographical references and index.
  ISBN 978-1-4166-2080-8 (pbk. : alk. paper) 1. Individualized instruction. I. Title.
  LB1031.T673 2015
  371.39'4–dc23
                                                            2015024914

24 23 22 21 20 19 18 17 16 15   1 2 3 4 5 6 7 8 9 10 11 12

LEADING for DIFFERENTIATION
Growing Teachers Who Grow Kids

Preface vii

1. So You (Might) Want to Lead for Differentiation? 1

2. Nurturing Individual Change 19

3. Designing a Vision for the Differentiated Landscape 43

4. Cultivating Deep Adult Learning 65

5. Engaging in Productive Conversations That Nourish Growth 87

6. Testing the Soil to Determine If
      Differentiation Is Making a Difference 109

7. Tending to Resistance That Pops Up 127

Conclusion: A Call to Lead for Lasting Growth 146

References 154

Index 158

About the Authors 163

Preface

That "differentiation" should be a fundamental part of contemporary classrooms is pervasively accepted. Professional groups such as the National Board of Professional Teaching Standards, the National Association for the Education of Young Children, the National Association of Elementary School Principals, the National Middle School Association, the National Association of Secondary School Principals, and the Council of Chief State School Officers profess the importance of effectively addressing learner variance in classrooms in order to promote academic success for the full range of students in contemporary schools. Teacher evaluation and development protocols such as Charlotte Danielson's (2013) *Framework for Teaching Evaluation Instrument*, the Tennessee Educator Acceleration Model Teacher Evaluation Rubrics, the Georgia Teacher Keys Effectiveness System, and the New York Approved Teacher Practice Rubrics are interwoven with the language and principles of differentiation as indicators of quality teaching. Nonetheless, indications are that robust differentiation is far from the norm in many, if not most, classrooms.

Implementation of differentiation requires a major shift in the thinking and habits of teachers. It represents what some experts (e.g., Fullan, 2007; Marzano, Waters, & McNulty, 2005; Waters, Marzano, & McNulty, 2003) refer to as "second-order change"—that is, it requires people to learn markedly new ways of doing their work, calling into question baseline assumptions and often creating a sense of unease or disruption in the process. In turn, that can cause people who have previously felt competent to suddenly feel inept at what they do. Thus, leadership for second-order change requires considerable skill and will on the part of the leader. Comprehensive change does not occur casually.

An earlier book, *The Differentiated School: Making Revolutionary Changes in Teaching and Learning* (Tomlinson, Brimijoin, & Narvaez, 2008), details the work of two public school principals—one elementary, one secondary—who successfully led schoolwide implementation of differentiation. Although the two schools were quite different in nature, and the two principals were equally different in leadership style, the principles and practices that guided their work were remarkably similar and mirrored the literature of successful change. *The Differentiated School* explores the thinking and actions of the two principals in the course of leading for broad implementation of differentiation in their schools. It also presents early and very positive achievement outcomes across the range of learners resulting from the change—a pattern that continued well beyond the years of the studies that served as the basis for the book.

The purpose of this book is to build on the earlier volume by providing a framework for mapping out and supporting change for differentiation so that leaders who choose to guide faculties to routinely provide responsive instruction in every classroom of the school will have ready access to practices and tools that support the process of this second-order change initiative. One of these tools, our Novice-to-Expert Rubric for Differentiation, is available for download on the ASCD website, along with the checklists for cultivating leadership competencies that conclude most chapters (enter this URL into your browser's search bar: www.ascd.org/ASCD/pdf/books/LeadingForDifferentiation.pdf, followed by the password *115005*.). In this way, the book is decidedly practical. Our intent, however, is also to provide enough of the "why" and "what" of leading for effective differentiated instruction so that the "how" is soundly informed. Examples of leaders who work from a shallow base of knowledge, understanding, and skill comprise a compendium of unsuccessful efforts.

The first chapter provides an opportunity to explore the "what" and "why" of leadership for schoolwide differentiation. We'll look first at why it is worth the effort of principals, specialists, and teachers to invest in differentiation, and then we'll examine the attributes of effective differentiation. The remainder of the book focuses on the "how."

Chapter 2 looks at the focal point of change in schools, factors that encourage teachers to change, and phases of long-term change. In

Chapter 3, we share a sound and fluid process for designing an operational vision for a differentiated school using powerful change plan conversations. Chapter 4 focuses on how professional development factors in achieving the vision of schoolwide differentiation. We provide tips on having great leader–teacher conversations in Chapter 5, including how to develop mindful listening skills. Chapter 6 focuses on distinguishing between assessment and evaluation, and suggests taking a *trifocal* view to better understand how teachers are implementing and reacting to the change for differentiation and how the school is progressing. Chapter 7 discusses the technical and social aspects of change and offers several useful strategies for managing resistance. To close the book, we share a story of an award-winning school superintendent who clearly exhibited the principles of leadership for change when he eliminated the tracking system in his district.

Overall, this work is a product of a "splendid beginning" resulting from a casual friendship that began for the two of us years ago. At first, our relationship was driven by a mutual passion for differentiation, equity, and the opportunity to explore those topics with educators at various settings in Texas. As time went on, however, we were able to work side by side with each other and with dedicated teachers and leaders as they grappled with the excitement and complexities of implementing differentiation in schools in a variety of locations. Ultimately, those shared experiences led us to a discussion about writing together. It began as a simple idea bantered about. As we discussed it more and more, our excitement level increased and a plan for collaborative authorship began to gel.

We are both motivated by working with schools whose leaders want to *do* the work of differentiation, not simply talk about it. The "why" and "what" of differentiation provide the bedrock on which our work stands. We hope to support leaders as they struggle with the leadership practices necessary to enact the principles and practices of differentiation across their schools.

Throughout the process of conceiving and writing the book, there have been several people whose support has been instrumental. Robbie Mitchell and the folks from the Greeneville City Schools (TN) provided an audience and fertile ground for many of the ideas in this book. The Greene County School District (TN), and especially its director, Vicki Kirk; the Webster Central School District (NY); the Round Rock Independent School District (TX); and the Tennessee Academy for School Leaders program all gave us opportunities to connect with leaders and share knowledge, skills, and tools. Lane Narvaez and Kay Brimijoin (Conway Elementary, MO) and Joyce Stone, Bill Rich, and Brad Blanchette (Colchester High, VT) have been both our teachers and sources of inspiration. From a distance, Carol Burris and Delia Garrity (Southside High, NY) and the various leaders of High Tech High (San Diego, CA) are our mentors as well. We hope we honor their work through what we share here. We also hope that, in the way books can teach, we have the opportunity to both challenge and inform the thinking of other leaders as these educators have challenged and informed ours.

—CAT/MM

1

So You (Might) Want to Lead for Differentiation?

There is no shortage of voices advocating for change in schools. Some of the causes and approaches are substantial, promising, and reflective of our best understanding of quality classroom practice. Some of the options are shallow, gimmicky, or ill-informed. Deciding on an initiative that merits the time and attention of faculty members as well as school leaders is a consequential decision. For the initiative to yield significant benefits for educators and students, the journey to success will involve mind-stretching, risk, awkwardness, and inconvenience for all involved. This is how it is with meaningful change. A wise leader carefully considers potential options for growth, and a wiser one recognizes the importance of choosing an option that is personally compelling. When you believe in the change you're proposing, it's easier to convince the people you lead that success is worth the hard work and occasional discomfort it will require.

Why Differentiation?

The model of differentiation we advocate is multifaceted—both rich and complex. It proposes that students achieve best in classrooms where teachers follow five key principles:

1. Offer each student a positive, secure, challenging, and supportive learning environment.

2. Provide a meaning-rich curriculum that is designed to engage learners and built around clearly articulated learning goals known to both teacher and students.

3. Use persistent formative assessment to ensure that teacher and students alike are aware of student status relative to the specified learning goals, and that teacher and students alike know what next steps are most likely to propel a given learner forward.

4. Plan instruction based on formative assessment information to attend to whole-class, small-group, and individual differences in readiness, interest, and approach to learning.

5. Work with students to create and implement classroom management routines that allow both predictability and flexibility.

This model of differentiation also emphasizes the interdependence of each of its five elements, reminding those who use it that, as is the case with all systems, the health of every element in the model predicts the health of every other element in the model.

We believe that developing a whole faculty's competence and confidence in differentiation is a worthy objective because it has the potential to improve the achievement of a full range of students in a school and the power to improve all aspects of classroom practice. Differentiation lifts the professional level of teachers by giving them both the opportunity and tools to chart pathways to success for all of the young people they serve. The scope and scale of a schoolwide differentiation change initiative is certainly ambitious, but it's exactly that comprehensiveness that opens the door to the greatest benefits (Fullan, 2001a).

Context has, or should have, much to do with undertaking a particular change initiative. A judicious leader should be able to say both privately and publicly, "This direction is important—in this place, at this time, for these teachers and students, and for these reasons." It seems a misappropriation of leadership to do less. The rationale for embarking on a particular change in a particular context also reflects the personality and educational perspectives of a particular leader.

For example, the elementary principal whose work was a focus in *The Differentiated School* (Tomlinson, et al., 2008) believed strongly that developing faculty expertise in differentiation would benefit all students in her school and would further professionalize an already dynamic faculty. This rationale guided her work and provided the basis for her appeal to the faculty to join her in that work. On the other hand, the high school principal spotlighted in *The Differentiated School* was propelled by her conviction that differentiation is a civil right. She saw two separate realities—two separate schools—in her building. In one, economically privileged students took advantage of high-quality course offerings, further improving their odds for a bright future. In the other, students with fewer economic means were consigned to low-track classes that made school dreary and their prospects for the future drearier. She felt deeply that differentiation was the key to creating a unified school in which the best curriculum and instruction would be accessible to virtually all students, and where advanced learners could find the enhanced challenge they needed. These two rationales for leading a schoolwide embrace of differentiation are certainly powerful, and each was appropriate for the leader and for the particular context.

We encourage you to examine *your* reasons for electing to invest in differentiation. They should be potent enough to fuel your work and the work of those you lead. At this point, we'd like to offer a few more rationales for leadership toward pervasive, high-quality differentiation—three rationales that were *not* the focus of either of the two principals in *The Differentiated School*. We present these not as a multiple-choice option—pick *a*, *b*, or *c*—but rather as a means of illustrating what we mean by "leading change from a sturdy platform."

Who's Coming to School? A Demographic Case for Differentiation

When we, the authors of this book, were making our way through K–12 classrooms, most of our classmates were from backgrounds relatively similar to our own in terms of ethnicity, language, family structure, and economics. Homogeneity was a myth that was more easily entertained than it is now. Students in today's classrooms are undeniably diverse, and look like a cross-section of life in all its aspects. Consider these realities:

• Slightly over 9 percent of students in the United States speak English as a second language (National Center for Education Statistics, 2014), although percentages vary by location and are as high as 23 percent of the population in many of the great city schools (Uro & Barrio, 2013).

• If we include students with limited English proficiency (LEP) in this tally, 13 percent of primary-grade students in U.S. public schools are less than proficient in English (National Center for Education Statistics, 2013).

- U.S. classrooms are more ethnically and culturally diverse today than at any time in the nation's past. In 2014, white students accounted for about 49.7 percent of the student population and no longer constituted the majority. Projections are that the percentage of white students will continue to decline, falling to about 45 percent by 2022 (Krogstad & Fry, 2014).
- About 5 percent of the U.S. school-age population has a diagnosed learning disability, with another 15 percent or more said to have learning or attention problems that remain undiagnosed. These students are at greater risk than the general population for failing a course in high school, not graduating from high school, and being suspended or expelled from school. Boys are about twice as likely to be diagnosed with a learning disability as girls (National Center for Learning Disabilities, 2014).
- In the United States, an estimated 13–20 percent of school-age young people have an emotional or mental health issue in a given year (Centers for Disease Control and Prevention, 2013).
- As many as 1 in 50 students has some form of autism spectrum disorder (about 2 percent of school-age children), with boys about 4 times more likely than girls to receive a diagnosis. This figure represents an increase of 72 percent in diagnosis since 2007—likely indicating better recognition of milder cases (Steenhuysen, 2013).
- Approximately 35–45 percent of students in U.S. public and charter schools in 2011–12 received Title I services provided for students who live in areas with high concentrations of low-income families (National Center for Education Statistics, 2013).
- Twenty-two percent of children in the United States live in poverty; 45 percent live in low-income families. Research suggests that poverty is associated with academic, social, emotional, and behavioral problems in children (National Center for Children in Poverty, 2014).
- Although national statistics are scarce on percentages of advanced learners in U.S. schools, it's likely that a sizeable segment of the school-age population is significantly underchallenged by current grade-level and standards-based curricula.

Although the idea of "a typical 5th grader" or a "standard issue 9th grader" has probably always been a construction of myth and convenience, today it seems delusional to operate from the premise that a one-size-fits-all approach to teaching will effectively address the range of learner needs in 21st century classrooms. Outside of school, these young people live in a world that enables them to customize a radio station, download single songs at any time, select from 52 flavors of ice cream, choose from among dozens of phone options and even more service plans, watch television and movies on demand, order burgers or bowls just as they'd like them, and select from hundreds of sports shoe designs. These same young people come to the classroom with a vast spectrum of educational entry points, bringing widely variable backgrounds, calling on disparate out-of-school support systems, fueled by different interests and dreams, and approaching learning in distinctly different ways. Both demographic evidence and sound logic make the case that learner differences should be in the forefront of teacher thinking and planning if our goal is maximum success for every student. All of our students depend on us to help them construct a solid academic foundation for life, and differentiated instruction is an approach that equips us for this responsibility.

What's the Evidence?
A Research-Based Case for Differentiation

Our model of differentiation, built on a positive learning environment, strong curriculum, formative assessment, instruction that responds to learner needs, and classroom leadership and management that balances predictability and flexibility in teaching and learning, reflects our best current understanding of the elements of quality classroom practice. There are, of course, many valid and reliable sources that distill current scholarship on teaching and learning. Some of these present findings from individual research studies that pinpoint the impact of particular aspects of teaching and learning. Others are meta-analyses that distill the work of many individual researchers to provide a "big picture" look at quality practice. When these latter sources are robust, they are incredibly helpful for practitioners, providing a level of guidance that would be almost impossible to construct on a teacher-by-teacher or school-by-school basis. Three that provide a particularly helpful scholarly and sound distillation of best practices are *How People Learn* (National Research Council, 2000) and two books by John Hattie: *Visible Learning* (2009) and *Visible Learning for Teachers* (2012).

How People Learn draws on research to make a case that effective classrooms are

• **Student-centered**, because to help each learner grow, it is imperative to know where that learner is in a progression from novice to competent to expert.

- **Knowledge-centered**, so that teachers and students invest in important learning goals that help learners make connections among ideas, see relationships among the various aspects of what they learn, and become able to apply and transfer what they learn to contexts beyond the immediate lesson and beyond the classroom.
- **Assessment-centered**, because effective use of formative assessment helps teacher and students better understand the student's learning journey and know how to construct the next steps in that journey.
- **Community-centered**, because it is important for students to have support as they grapple with challenge and because working in a community (rather than in isolation) inevitably models varied pathways to learning.

These four traits of effective classrooms relate directly to four of the five key principles of differentiation: positive learning environment, powerful curriculum, consistent use of formative assessment, and responsive instruction designed to ensure consistent growth for each student. The idea of a community-centered classroom also overlaps with important elements in the fifth principle of differentiation: teacher and students joining together to make the classroom work for everyone.

The work of John Hattie is arguably the most significant examination of the past several decades of research on student achievement. Hattie's goal was to examine all available studies that address the question of which teacher practices contribute most to student achievement. In *Visible Learning* (2009), he details the findings of his work—a meta-analysis of more than 800 other meta-analyses, covering 50,000 studies and more than 200 million students. In *Visible Learning for Teachers* (2012), Hattie translates those findings into specific guidance for both teachers and those who seek to support teachers in developing the most effective practices possible.

The scope of Hattie's work is impressive, to say the least, and capsuling all of his findings that relate directly to the model of differentiation we advocate is well beyond the scope of this chapter. Nonetheless, it is useful to note at least a few conclusions from Hattie's research synthesis, as they map directly onto practices that are central to our perception of effectively differentiated classrooms.

Among practices he advocates as beneficial for student achievement and, therefore, important in classrooms are classroom management that facilitates learning, classroom environments that reduce anxiety, student engagement with content and learning, motivation that stems from the students feeling in charge of their learning, and small-group learning in which materials vary to match the needs of students in the groups. Practices Hattie reports to be even more productive in terms of student achievement include setting challenging goals (directly related to the differentiation concept of "teaching up"), classroom cohesion, and peer tutoring.

Still more impressive in terms of positive student outcomes are *not* labeling students, using a wide variety of teaching strategies, and using collaborative rather than individualistic learning. Finally, among practices that resulted in the highest gains in student achievement are consistent use of formative assessment with quality feedback to students and supportive teacher–student relationships.

Briefly, here are few conclusions from Hattie's work that not only align with important principles of differentiation but also point to the interrelatedness of those principles.

Invitational Learning Environments. Hattie writes that environments that lead to achievement for all students are "invitational," or characterized by a transparent commitment to the learning of every student and a consideration of what each student brings to the lesson. Such environments encourage students to be collaborative partners in their own learning. Teachers in invitational environments demonstrate *respect* (the belief that every student is able, valuable, and responsible), *trust* (they work collaboratively with students to ensure that learning is engaging and that the process of learning is as important as the product of learning), *optimism* (students get an unambiguous message that they have the potential necessary to learn what is required), and *intentionality* (it's clear that every step in the lesson was designed to invite every student to learn and to succeed). Teachers in invitational environments believe that their students' intelligence is fluid rather than fixed.

Student-Centered Teachers. These teachers visibly demonstrate (not just intend) warmth for each student through unconditional respect and positive regard. They exhibit belief in students, especially when the student is struggling. They are empathetic, understanding that students will learn in many different ways, and they make it a habit to put themselves in each student's shoes in an effort to grasp which approaches will work best to move that student forward. They have a positive relationship with their students—perhaps a reflection of their high expectations, warmth, and encouragement.

Respectful Environments and Well-Managed Classrooms. Classes with student-centered teachers exhibit more student engagement, fewer negative behaviors, more student-initiated and student-regulated activities, and higher achievement outcomes.

Student Motivation. Student motivation is highest when students are competent, have sufficient autonomy, set worthwhile goals, get useful feedback, have a sense of control over their own learning, and are affirmed by others.

Attention to Student Learning Differences. Cognitive development advances on its own schedule. Students' readiness to engage in various stages of thinking isn't directly tied to age, follows no strict learning sequence, and varies across content areas. This calls on teachers to study their students and act on what they learn. Teachers must know what students already know and how they think and then craft lessons to move all students forward according to the criteria for success. Teachers should aspire to know what each and every student is thinking and grasping, to construct meaningful learning experiences in light of this knowledge, and to know their content deeply enough to be able to provide feedback that will guide each student through curriculum progressions.

Instruction Informed by Formative Assessment. Expert teachers monitor learning, provide feedback, and adapt their instruction as needed. Evidence doesn't provide teachers with rules for follow-up action but rather with hypotheses for intelligent problem solving. Thus, teachers must ask themselves what works best, for whom, and compared to what alternatives. Asking only, "What works?" can be limiting. The critical nature of teachers' judgment and decision-making skills points to the need for a caring relationship with and among students.

Deep Curricular Understanding and Differentiation. Expert teachers teach at a deep (versus surface) level of knowledge more consistently than teachers who are not as proficient. They also have very clear learning goals for each lesson, know how well the various students are reaching criteria for success, and know their content well enough to select the best "next step" to span the gap between a student's current knowledge and criteria for success.

In *Visible Learning for Teachers*, Hattie (2012) speaks directly and insightfully to differentiation, noting that because successful instruction depends on teachers knowing where students are and moving them forward from those points, trying to teach to the class as a whole will lead to an instructional mismatch for many:

> This is where the skill of teachers in knowing the similarities across students and allowing for the differences becomes so important. Differentiation relates primarily to structuring classes so that all students are working "at or +1" from

where they start, such that all can have maximal opportunities to attain the success criteria of the lessons.... [D]ifferentiation relates more to the phases of learning—from novice, through capable, to proficient—rather than merely providing different activities to different (groups of) students.

For differentiation to be effective, teachers need to know, for each student, where the student begins and where he or she is in his or her journey towards meeting the criteria of the lesson. Is the student a novice, somewhat capable, or proficient? What are his or her strengths and gaps in knowledge and understanding? What learning strategies does he or she have and how can we help him or her to develop other useful learning strategies? Depending on the student's phase of learning, their understanding of surface and deep thinking, their phase of motivation, and their strategies of learning, the teacher will have to provide different ways in which students can demonstrate mastery and understanding along the way to meeting the success criteria. It should be obvious why rapid formative feedback can be so powerful for teachers to know [a student's] phase of learning and then help [him or her] to achieve "+1" outcomes.

The key is for teachers to have a clear reason for differentiation and to relate what they do differently to where the student is located on the progression from novice to expert relative to the learning goals and criteria for success. In grouping students, the goal is not necessarily to arrange students by place in the learning progression, but rather to group students at varied places in the progression so students can move forward as they discuss with, work with, and see the world through the eyes of other students. (pp. 109–110)

Hattie goes on to point out that "the mistake is to assume that just because students 'sit in groups,' there is learning in groups" (p. 110)—or that differentiation is occurring. Differentiation requires structure and instruction designed to help students develop the skills necessary to learn in groups.

The multifaceted and complex nature of differentiation makes it difficult for researchers to study as a whole model. What's more, it is a "generalist" model, and much research is conducted in specialty areas (e.g., special education, gifted education, multicultural education, English language learning, and reading). Nonetheless, in excess of 25 studies have been conducted in recent years examining the effect of differentiation as a generic model on student achievement, with findings largely positive. Those studies are reviewed in other publications (e.g., Tomlinson et al., 2003; Tomlinson & Imbeau, 2013; Tomlinson & McTighe, 2006). Additionally, numerous studies conducted in specialized areas of education such as reading and special education examine the effects of differentiation on student achievement; again, these studies revealed largely positive outcomes.

It is our strong belief that learning to differentiate effectively is learning to teach at an expert level. It is at the core of quality teaching, not an addendum to it. There is ample basis, in the theory and research of education, to warrant the investment of teacher effort and the support from leaders necessary to enable more teachers to respond to learner differences in ways that multiply achievement across the spectrum of students in contemporary classrooms. It is important for those who seek to provide teacher support for differentiation to understand its research-based justification.

Which Way Is North?
The Ethical Case for Differentiation

Noted businessman and motivational speaker Stephen Covey sometimes asks members of an audience to stand, close their eyes, and point to the north. When all the hands are raised and index fingers pointing, he asks participants to keep their arms raised and fingers pointing while opening their eyes. The response is predictably explosive laughter. There seems no consensus at all on compass points, with numerous people pointing up, down, left, right, and diagonally. Covey uses the moment to make the point that if we don't have an ethical North in life, we'll always be adrift.

Psychologists who study moral development (e.g., Kohlberg, 1981; Piaget, 1997) suggest that individuals may develop in moral "sophistication" over time—perhaps beginning with a rule-following orientation, moving toward moral reasoning based on self-interest, progressing to morality based on what the group is doing or what others will think, growing to decisions based on what will best serve the group, and perhaps ultimately acting out of a conviction that something is right—even if the decision negates rules, self-interest, the will of the group, and so on. Although there is not universal agreement on validity of these specific stages and how they progress, this progression at least calls our attention to the possibility that people can move away from an egocentric orientation to the world toward a more expansive view of right and wrong.

It is instructive to pose Stephen Covey's question about an ethical North in the context of progressions of moral development as they might apply to the decision making of educators, both individually and as a group. How often do we make decisions based on rules, personal preference, or the press of the group rather than on what will best serve students or the profession or a nation or the world? Noted educator Lorna

Earl (2003) seems to point to the importance of the two "higher" stages of moral decision making when she makes the assertion that it is the overriding moral purpose of the teacher to meet students' needs, even when that decision conflicts with personal preferences.

It seems evident that contemporary classrooms are populated by students whose backgrounds, experiences, and needs are characterized by diversity. There is also generous evidence that student-focused approaches to teaching and learning result in greater achievement for the full range of students than do more uniform or rigid approaches. In the past, educators in the United States have acknowledged student differences and the need to address them largely by calling for tracking or "ability grouping." It is common to hear the explanation that such arrangements enable teachers to do a better job of "teaching where students are," enabling them to address student learning needs more effectively.

Although there is little if any research on any topic in education that provides indisputable findings, there are tomes of studies on the efficacy of ability grouping; most of these suggest that ability grouping is disadvantageous to students in the low and middle tracks and perhaps advantageous to students in the upper tracks, although more recent research (e.g., Marsh, Tautwein, Ludtke, Baumert, & Koller, 2007) calls the latter conclusion into question. It has been reconfirmed many times that students in low tracks are likely to have newer or weaker teachers while students in the high tracks are more likely to have expert-level teachers. Likewise, high tracks are typically characterized by high expectations, while low tracks are marked by low expectations.

Haberman (1991) describes low-track instruction as a "pedagogy of poverty," injecting into the discussion of "ability grouping" or tracking   the issue of economics and race. He notes that low-track classes are disproportionally made up of students from low-income or racial-minority groups and are marked by low-level tasks, rote work, giving and repeating information, and student noncompliance. He explains that he chose the phrase "pedagogy of poverty" because the preponderance of students in these classes are poor, and the nature of the classes seems designed to ensure continuation of that status.

Hodges (2001), by contrast, writes about what she calls a "pedagogy of plenty"—classes predominantly populated by more affluent students and characterized by meaningful knowledge, robust dialogue, purposeful activities, quality resources, and problem solving. Echoing Haberman, she notes that the phrase "pedagogy of plenty" not only describes the economic status of most students in such classes but also predicts future outcomes for students who benefit from long-term involvement with the classes.

The history of education in the United States is punctuated with cycles of favoring "ability grouping," or tracking, to attend to student variance followed by cycles in which evidence against that practice dominates the conversation. In the latter instance, educators eschew ability grouping and place most students in heterogeneous classes for much, if not all, of their learning. Unfortunately, when we do that, we typically fail to attend to the student differences that typify heterogeneity—varied readiness levels, interests, and approaches to learning. Predictably, then, heterogeneity is dismissed as ineffective, and we once again migrate back to "homogeneity" in grouping students.

In the United States, educators have not, in any meaningful way, embraced the third grouping option—that is, proliferating heterogeneous classrooms in which we both "teach up" and differentiate instruction to enable most students to succeed with meaning-rich and relevant curriculum. Yet we have among us, or could learn, the skills necessary to create a pedagogy of plenty—that is, to develop high-end curriculum and deliver the kind of learning experiences often reserved for a small percentage of students whom we deem able to benefit from it. We have among us, or could learn, the skills necessary to "differentiate up"—that is, to scaffold learning for students who are not currently succeeding in school to enable them to access complex, meaning-rich learning. Arguably, the current emphasis on Common Core standards, complex Common Core–like standards, and 21st century skills provides even greater support for the expectation that virtually all of our students should and can succeed with what we have often thought of as "advanced" curriculum.

If educators have, or could develop, the skills necessary to "teach up" and "differentiate up," the question that remains is whether we have the moral will to invest in that decision. One of John Hattie's conclusions is that labeling students is a detriment to learning, and he is among many experts who draw this conclusion. Van Manen (1986), for example, reminds us of the danger inherent in seeing students as anything less than unique individuals:

> Once I call a child "a behavior problem" or a "low achiever," or once I refer to him as someone who has a specific learning style, a particular mode of cognitive functioning, then I am immediately inclined to reach into my portfolio of instructional tricks for a specific instructional intervention. What happens then

is that I forego the possibility of truly listening to or seeing the specific child. Instead, I put the child away in categorical language, as constraining as a real prison. Putting children away by means of technical or instrumental language is really a kind of spiritual abandonment. (p. 18)

A leader willing to support the schoolwide embrace of more responsive instruction would be wise to examine, and lead faculty in examining, which students in a school are in low-level classes and how often participation in those classes results in students "moving up" academically; which students benefit from the highest quality curriculum we know how to create and which students regularly experience something less; which students are surrounded with vibrant and diverse peer perspectives and which students hear only echoes of themselves; and which labeling and grouping practices dignify students and which of these discourage students in some significant way.

In a democratic society and based on our best knowledge of quality teaching, there is a strong ethical imperative to differentiate instruction in the context of heterogeneous classrooms. Strong leaders have the opportunity to help colleagues establish and follow an ethical North.

The "What" of Effective Differentiation

It is likely unwise for a principal or district leader to take on the role of chief professional developer for differentiation. That role is best left for a well-qualified educator who has experience and a solid understanding of differentiation, or a designated school leader who has similar experience and understanding as well as dedicated time to work with colleagues both in and out of their classrooms (Tomlinson et al., 2008). Nonetheless, building and district leaders who seek to ensure teacher growth in responsive teaching will necessarily be differentiation planners, assessors, discussants, and coaches. It is not possible to play those roles responsibly without a comprehensive and accurate understanding of differentiation.

Teachers who differentiate instruction effectively craft an environment that signals the value of each individual, provides high challenge with high support, and emphasizes the power of community in achieving success for every learner. They clarify what students must *know*, *understand*, and be able to *do* (KUDs) in order to develop proficiency in a topic or content area. They plan lessons designed to be relevant and engaging to their students—both individually and as a group. They continually monitor student growth relative to KUDs, and they provide feedback and design instruction based on what they learn about student development from systematic interaction with each student, classroom observation, and formative assessment data. Finally, teachers who differentiate instruction enlist the partnership of their students in developing and implementing classroom routines that facilitate their ability to address both whole-class and individual needs.

This environment is the essence of classroom differentiation. It's also a powerful platform for thinking about and planning to lead a faculty to become competent and confident differentiators. The leader, then, takes on the role of teacher. He or she must create an environment in which each teacher feels valued, challenged, supported, and part of a team working together for success. The leader must be clear about what *teachers* should know, understand, and be able to do in order to differentiate instruction skillfully. He or she must continually monitor teacher growth toward these KUDs, providing feedback and developing learning opportunities for teachers based on their varied readiness levels, interests, and approaches to teaching and learning. Then the leader creates structures designed to ensure that each teacher progresses in facility and comfort with addressing learner needs. This means he or she must sometimes work with the faculty as a whole, sometimes work with small groups, and sometimes work with individuals.

When leading any long-term change initiative, it is helpful to use principles of "backward design" (Wiggins & McTighe, 2005). In broad terms, the leader identifies the essential knowledge, understanding, and skills that are necessary for learner (teacher) success. Then the leader determines what major summative benchmarks will indicate teacher success with the KUDs or with specific subsets of the KUDs. Finally, the leader plans learning experiences designed to help teachers master the KUDs so that there is a high likelihood of teacher competence with the summative benchmarks. A part of this third element in backward design is use of persistent formative assessment (in the form of classroom observations, lesson plan analysis, analysis of video lessons, planning conversations, etc.) to inform the next steps of both the leader and the teacher. This deceptively simple, three-stage planning approach is remarkably powerful in ensuring leader and teacher clarity about goals and expectations and in aligning learning opportunities with intended outcomes.

Many aspects of a long-term plan for differentiation will vary across sites. It is helpful, however, to have a resource that can guide your thinking about the key attributes of effective differentiation—KUDs that will clarify goals for individuals and the faculty as a whole, establish targets for both formative and summative assessment, and frame professional learning opportunities. Figure 1.1 offers a reasonable starting point for defining the KUDs necessary for competence with differentiation.

FIGURE 1.1

Key Learning Targets (KUDs) for Teacher Proficiency with Differentiation

Know	Understand	Do
• Five key elements of differentiation • Mindset • Know-Understand-Do (KUDs for students) • Engagement • Understanding • Alignment • Ongoing assessment (pre-assessment, formative, summative) • Flexible grouping • Respectful tasks • Readiness, interest, learning profile • Cultural responsiveness • Teaching up • Instructional strategies for differentiation • Equity and excellence	• Differentiation is a philosophy and not simply a set of strategies. • Differentiation is designed to maximize the capacity of each learner. • Mindset shapes teaching and learning. • Teacher connection with kids opens them up to the risk of learning. • Community commitment multiplies support for students and the teacher. • Ongoing assessment guides quality differentiation. • The quality of what we teach contributes to the impact of how we teach—and vice versa. • Flexible classroom routines balance group and individual needs.	• Reflect on philosophy and practice. • Create and maintain an invitational learning environment. • Develop KUD frameworks, drawing on standards. • Develop formative assessments aligned with KUDs. • Interpret assessment results to determine students' learning needs. • Develop differentiated tasks based on assessment information in response to student readiness, interest, and learning profile. • Work with students to understand differentiation and establish flexible plans for it.

Figure 1.2 provides a tool for thinking about teacher development along a continuum of knowledge, understanding, and skill with each of the five key elements of differentiation: positive learning environment, strong curriculum, formative assessment, instruction that responds to learner needs, and classroom leadership and management that balances the need for predictability and flexibility in teaching and learning. We encourage you to use both of these tools as frameworks for early thinking and planning, with the understanding that these frameworks will evolve as leader and teacher expertise develops.

FIGURE 1.2

A Novice-to-Expert Continuum to Guide Thinking About Teacher Development with Key Differentiation Elements

Element	Less Developed			Well Developed
Environment	Flat affect with students evident	Student-awareness evident	General emotional support for students evident	Student–teacher partnership evident
	Fixed mindset evident	Belief in the capacity of wider range of students evident	Growth mindset generally evident	Growth mindset evident
	Few teacher–student connections evident	Connections with students evident	Community-building evident	Class functions as a team
Curriculum	Fact/skill-based	Some emphasis on understanding	Understandings included	Understanding–focused
	Low goal clarity	Some use of articulated goals	Generally clear KUDs	KUDs clear to students/ teacher
	Coverage-driven	Some planning for relevance	General attention to relevance	Planned for high relevance and for "teaching up"
Assessment	*Of* learning	*For* learning	*For* learning	*For* and *as* learning
	Low alignment with KUDs	Better alignment with KUDs	Tight alignment with KUDs	Authentic
	Fact/skill-based	More emphasis on understanding	Understandings often in the foreground	Focused feedback and differentiated assessments
Instruction	One size fits all, with little or no differentiation	Choice as differentiation/ reactive differentiation	Interest/learning profile emphasized	Readiness emphasized
	Some alignment with state goals evident	General alignment with KUDs	Clear KUDs, with understanding emphasized	Clear KUDs, consistent emphasis on meaning making
	Little student collaboration or movement	Some use of groups, often random or "ability"-based	Some attention to flexible grouping and respectful tasks	Consistent use of flexible grouping and respectful tasks
Classroom Leadership and Management	Compliance-focused			Philosophy-guided
	Rule-oriented			Learning-oriented
	Low trust of students			Student voice and responsibility prioritized
	Focused on managing kids			Focused on leading kids and managing routines

Preparing to Lead for More Responsive Classrooms

It can take a long time for meaningful differentiation to take root and flourish. Throughout the process, teachers will have to give up some familiar and comfortable ideas and practices. They will have to learn to see students and their responsibility to students in new ways. Odds are that growth will be uneven at times; it may slow or even reverse for a while. When and if this occurs, the leader's best recourse is to remain grounded in the intent to improve the lives of teachers and students through differentiation, to know differentiation's tenets and practices deeply, and to embody and model differentiation in his or her own practice.

Leading for schoolwide differentiation requires leaders to enlist the minds and hearts of teachers in understanding and ultimately accepting the premise that to respect students is to serve each of them. They must learn to trust in every student's capacity to grapple with profound ideas and complex skills and provide all students the level of support they need to become what they should. Schoolwide differentiation requires leaders who know their ethical North—leaders who will establish "covenant relationships" with teachers, indicating shared commitment to an important purpose (Sergiovanni, 1992).

Leading for differentiation requires leaders to work with teachers collegially, understanding the difference between "power to" and "power over"—exercising "moral leadership" rather than "command leadership" (Sergiovanni, 1992). It summons leaders to work with teachers to develop the vision for student-focused instruction so that a way forward is clear. It necessitates that leaders provide teachers with the sustained support necessary to grow steadily from a current point of proficiency while attending to students' varied learning needs as they progress toward expertise. It asks leaders to use formative assessment to guide their thinking and planning and to help teachers develop growing agency in their work. It needs leaders who celebrate significant victories and who challenge unproductive and unsuccessful approaches.

In the end, leading for schoolwide differentiation challenges leaders as absolutely as it challenges teachers. It also holds as much promise for leaders to hone their leadership skills as it does for teachers to hone their pedagogical skills. Most of all, it provides an opportunity for leaders and teachers to honor what should be the promise of every school for every young person who enters its doors: *We see you, we hold you in high regard, and we will give ourselves to your success as a learner and as a human being.*

This chapter has briefly explored the "why" and "what" of differentiation. The remainder of the book will provide a guide for becoming an effective catalyst for it. We will map out how to lead significant, school-wide change to embrace high-quality instruction for the full range of learners for the purpose of ensuring that each student has equal access to excellent learning opportunities and the support he or she needs to succeed with the essential goals of those opportunities.

2

Nurturing Individual Change

Having explored the "why" of a move toward schoolwide differentiation and some of the elements of differentiation that will be useful when planning for professional growth, goal setting, coaching, and the formative and summative evaluation of the change process, it's time to take a close look at the "how." How can we, as school leaders, think about, plan for, and support second-order change that will result in instruction that is responsive to the full range of learner needs within a classroom?

In this chapter, we'll look at factors that encourage teachers to change and that support change in teachers, and at the phases of long-term change that predictably occur when teachers across a school undertake a significant new initiative. These ideas provide a foundation for the other aspects of leadership for change that follow in the remainder of the book.

Do *Schools* Change, or Do People?

Thinking about this question means considering the interplay of relationships and results that accompany the launch of significant new initiatives. When we first contemplate a big, fundamental work like a differentiated approach to instruction, the scale of the change we are seeking can be overwhelming. These kinds of changes, sometimes called second-order change (e.g., Fullan, 2001a), are profound and, if fully institutionalized, will manifest in all aspects of schooling.

To cultivate the kinds of deep changes necessary to really alter and enhance quality teaching and learning, we must orchestrate a set of actions and supports that *allow and expect* teachers to grow in their expertise. This process requires a shift *away* from thinking of the school as the target of improvement (traditional thinking) and toward individual teacher development. To put it more succinctly, schools don't change; the individuals within schools must change their practices (Hall & Hord, 2001). If schools are more and more successful, it is because the individuals within the school walls are working in conditions that support their own development, build the relationships they have with one another, and hold one another accountable for improvement, day by day. In other words, *the individuals* in schools should be the focus of change efforts. Change happens person by person, or it does not happen.

School leaders swamped with data and initiatives may be seduced into believing that the act of writing complicated action plans will somehow lead to better student outcomes. This never works. The leader's vision, accompanied by a dogged determination for results, is where real change starts—and this determination must then spread to the *people* who work in the school. It is constant effort invested in building professional relationships along with constant examination of results that enables teacher growth. And support for *teacher* change is a precursor to *student* change. As a principal friend, Vaughn Gross, aptly put it, bringing about significant teacher change requires a "shove and a hug." That philosophy represents the real call to action for school leaders, asking us to focus squarely on growing people while we keep an eye on the vision and the results. In other words, this kind of change calls on all who lead school change to apply pressure as well as to build capacity.

The focus on relationships is not to be taken lightly. Time after time, conversations with decision makers in successful organizations circle back to the high value they place on the relationships they help build among people. If leaders want positive outcomes, they must cultivate positive and constructive relationships that consistently provide information necessary for making critical decisions. More succinctly, to create new solutions for increasingly challenging problems, we *have to have* these relationships in order to enlist the ability and creativity of the people in our schools. Toxic relationships diminish capacity (Lewin & Regine, 1999). "Neutral relationships" are no help either.

With so much emphasis on massive district and school initiatives, it may very well be that we are the victims of our own hard work. Under the weight of enormous outside pressures for accelerated school change, we may comfort ourselves with the feeling that as long as we feel busy, we must be doing important things. Unfortunately, this "doing things" philosophy often focuses us on managing tidbits of the initiative and sacrificing the central need to retain powerful and instructive relationships with the individuals we must count on to lead the changes in their classrooms.

Across the United States and in many parts of the world, districts and schools are launching initiatives to implement differentiated instruction in all classrooms. Often, the initiatives reflect a need and desire to support the success of increasingly diverse student populations who need to succeed with complex, mandated curriculum standards. The idea of "growing teachers who grow kids" logically positions differentiation as key to robust growth for a full range of learners. To achieve that worthy goal, we must keep in mind the reality that cultivating effectively differentiated classroom practice requires us to focus the significant changes through the lens of each individual teacher and to *live* differentiated leadership that supports individual teachers as they develop the skills of responsive instruction.

What *Doesn't* Motivate People to Change and Develop?

As school leaders, we may not know where to start to grow individual teachers in a strategic, relationship-based way. We suggest that these efforts must begin with clarity about what motivates people to develop and reflect on their professional practices. An understanding of why teachers are willing to work toward continuous improvement should inform the daily actions of leaders who seek to both support growth in their colleagues and hold them accountable for their individual development. Consider the following case study, which has played out countless times in schools.

....

Unintentionally "Demotivating" Veronica Simpson

Veronica Simpson is a 7th grade language arts teacher with five years of successful experience. She works in an urban middle school in the Midwest. She is a conscientious and dedicated professional who enjoys a solid relationship with her principal, Deborah Jefferson. Over the current school year, Ms. Jefferson has been in Ms. Simpson's classroom three times—twice for short walkthrough visits and once for the longer, formal observation. As a result of these three visits, Ms. Jefferson has noticed a few instructional areas where Ms. Simpson might improve. She is eager to meet with Ms. Simpson to offer some feedback and suggestions. In fact, she has already contacted a fellow teacher, Mrs. Austin, to see if Ms. Simpson might visit her classroom and learn from how Mrs. Austin handles a few of the issues that are a struggle for this teacher.

Ms. Jefferson conducts the meeting with Ms. Simpson in a professional and supportive conference. She offers plenty of praise for the things Ms. Simpson does well. When it comes time to focus on areas for professional improvement, Ms. Jefferson brings up the idea of observing Mrs. Austin, stressing how beneficial it will be and explaining that she herself will "cover" Ms. Simpson's class during this time. The visit to Mrs. Austin's class is scheduled, and the feedback conference concludes with Ms. Simpson communicating that she appreciates her principal's guidance and looks forward to improving her practice.

When left alone, however, Ms. Simpson has a strange sense of discontent… and a nagging sense of discouragement. Although she agrees with the growth areas pointed out to her and definitely wants to be a more successful teacher, she really doesn't want to visit Mrs. Austin's classroom. Why is she having these feelings? Why is she reluctant to see Mrs. Austin's methods and talk with her about improvement?

In this scenario, we see a principal who went into a conversation with the best intentions and deployed a common teacher growth strategy. So why did this approach backfire, leaving the teacher "de-motivated" rather than excited to pursue new learning and develop new skills?

The mistakes Ms. Jefferson made are typical ones, according to *Crucial Accountability* (Patterson, Grenny, Maxfield, McMillan, & Switzler, 2013). Her first error was to rely on charisma and try to leverage her good, personal relationship with Ms. Simpson into motivation. Her second was to use power. When a supervisor makes a suggestion to a supervised employee, that suggestion is essentially a "soft command." But Ms. Jefferson's main error in change leadership can be summed up as a failure to leverage what research tells us really propels people to embrace growth and development: *intrinsic motivation.* Although her "request" to Ms. Simpson was delivered with good intentions, it was at best an external motivator: "Do this because I (the leader) think it's a good idea, and it will please me." Ms. Simpson took action primarily because her boss told her to. She felt compelled to visit Mrs. Austin's classroom because that was the course of action presented to her rather than because of her own belief that she needed to improve certain elements of her practice. Observing Mrs. Austin's methods may (or may not) result in some short-term gains in Ms. Simpson's performance, but it is doubtful that this alone will trigger intrinsic motivation to grow. Unless Ms. Jefferson alters her approach to leading change, Ms. Simpson is unlikely to take further steps in her development unless and until she receives further external pressure. Thus her development is minimal and dependent on an "external irritant" to keep her motivated.

Although there are rare cases when this kind of external direction is needed with teachers who may be reluctant or afraid to change, as leaders we are far more effective when we focus on elements of motivation that compel and support teachers to act on an *internal* "drive" to continuously develop.

Dig Deep: Right now, how would you describe your approach for leading big changes? Is your approach balanced in terms of building relationships *and* focusing on results? Would others describe your approach to change the same way you would? Why or why not? Do you often "sell" your changes by focusing on things that don't intrinsically motivate people? How would you honestly assess your methods?

What Motivational Factors Help to Cultivate Teacher Growth?

Daniel H. Pink's book *Drive* (2009) provides a deceptively simple framework for thinking about motivation and individuals. It mirrors the noted work of Edward Deci and his colleague Richard Flaste, summarized for a lay audience in *Why We Do What We Do: Understanding Self-Motivation* (1996). Pink proposes three key elements in positive motivation: autonomy, purpose, and mastery. Deci and Flaste suggest three elements as well: autonomy, competence, and connectedness. The concept of autonomy appears in both models, and mastery and competence are synonymous.

Our experience suggests that in addition to the two elements common to both models, people are motivated to change in positive and authentic ways when they come to deeply understand the reason for a change (purpose—Pink, 2009) and when they feel related to others in the process of becoming autonomous and skilled (connectedness—Deci &

Flaste, 1996). Thus we believe all of these elements are critical for effective leadership for change. Simply put, meaningful change will not occur unless those who must do the changing are motivated to change.

Throughout this book we adhere to the notion that real change is collaborative and should connect practitioners and leaders in focused and supportive work; in Chapter 5, we will specifically look at how leaders can build connectedness with and among faculty and why connectedness matters to support meaningful and enduring change. At the moment, though, we're concerned with the roles that **autonomy**, **purpose**, and **mastery/competence** play in motivating individuals to embrace change in school settings. This understanding of basic motivation theory helps us as leaders refocus the way we approach the challenge of growing teachers in order to grow kids.

Autonomy

Autonomy is perhaps the most important motivator for people; indeed, the more we learn about motivation, the more we move away from categorizing behavior as either extrinsically motivated or intrinsically motivated and consider instead whether or not the behavior was "controlled" or "autonomous" (Stone, Deci, & Ryan, 2009). Autonomy is not necessarily "independence." It is, instead, the idea of acting with choice. Stone, Deci, and Ryan point out that individuals can be autonomous and still interdependent with others. In fact, autonomy resides in a creative tension between the need to be in control and exercise freedom, and at the same time, the desire to belong to a community of appreciation, support, and cooperation (Tschannen-Moran & Tschannen-Moran, 2010).

Inherent in the idea of autonomy is the notion that, in schools, communication among the principal and teachers is rich and full of meaningful feedback and idea exchange, information is full and continuous, and the school leaders lay out significant choices while encouraging teachers to take on the new challenges. Different from "empowerment"—which can simply be a more civilized form of control—autonomy must be considered along four aspects (Pink, 2009). In Figure 2.1, consider how each aspect influences an individual's perception of autonomy within the context of the school setting, the work, the quality of relationships, and a team approach to improvement.

Although they are represented in the figure as a "flow," it's also important to remember that all of the elements are interconnected. The degree of intensity and urgency of each element is unique to a specific context.

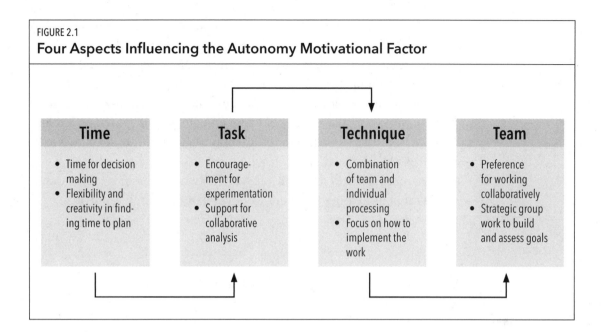

FIGURE 2.1
Four Aspects Influencing the Autonomy Motivational Factor

Time	Task	Technique	Team
• Time for decision making • Flexibility and creativity in finding time to plan	• Encouragement for experimentation • Support for collaborative analysis	• Combination of team and individual processing • Focus on how to implement the work	• Preference for working collaboratively • Strategic group work to build and assess goals

As leaders, we must consider the four elements as they exist in our particular setting and determine the degree of autonomy our teachers *must* feel to remain focused on and propelled through the differentiation work.

Purpose

A second element in motivation is **purpose**. As Pink (2009) puts it, "The most deeply motivated people—not to mention those who are most productive and satisfied—hitch their desires to a cause larger than themselves" (p. 131). In schools, this idea translates to the notion that the primary goal is not gains in student scores but positioning students to be successful individuals in the world. One "profit" may be higher test scores—a kind of recognition that may propel teachers to continue developing and pursuing teaching strategies to continue this trend—but the purpose is higher, deeper, and more "moral" (Pink, 2009). Fullan (2001a) describes this moral sense in two ways: (1) the difference we want to make in others' lives, and (2) the way we go about doing that work. In this way, then, purpose is about the passion we garner and the processes we use to create better conditions for others.

School leaders are critical advocates in helping individual teachers understand their purpose. "[Teachers] need to work in schools in which leadership is supportive, clear, strong and passionately committed to maintaining the quality of their commitment" (Chris Day, as quoted in Hargreaves & Fullan, 2012, p. 62). This role calls on us to clearly and consistently articulate the vision for differentiation, to be unbending in our commitment to its purpose, and to steadily build consensus about both the vision and means for achieving it. To build and sustain commitment to differentiation as a core school value and classroom practice, leaders talk about it, model it, organize for it, support it, insist on it, celebrate it, and express keen dissatisfaction when actions betray the shared value (Sergiovanni, 1992). Figure 2.2 illustrates two necessary factors that assist leaders in helping teachers to develop and maintain purpose.

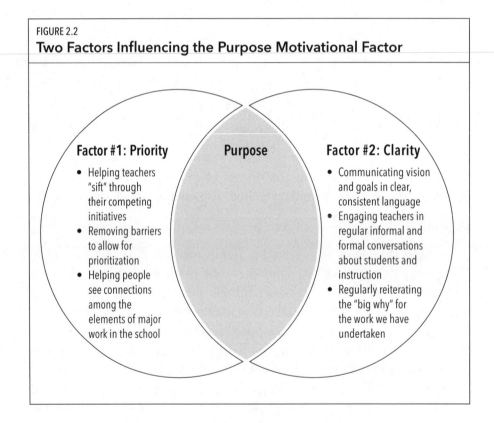

FIGURE 2.2
Two Factors Influencing the Purpose Motivational Factor

Factor #1: Priority
- Helping teachers "sift" through their competing initiatives
- Removing barriers to allow for prioritization
- Helping people see connections among the elements of major work in the school

Purpose

Factor #2: Clarity
- Communicating vision and goals in clear, consistent language
- Engaging teachers in regular informal and formal conversations about students and instruction
- Regularly reiterating the "big why" for the work we have undertaken

Mastery

A third motivation element is **mastery** (Pink, 2009). Mastery is directly connected to the idea of efficacy in that, as individuals, we believe that we *can* continue to get better at things. In other words, mastery is the belief in the journey and in the idea that each of our developmental journeys can continue to increase and deepen instead of ending because of personal limits.

In her book *Mindset*, Carol Dweck (2006) connects these ideas of mastery to two views of how people think about success in themselves and in others. People with a "fixed" mindset believe that the capacity to grow is limited by heredity and environment and cannot be significantly increased. These individuals also place great value in "performance goals" such as getting a reward for efforts or achieving some kind of recognized status. By contrast, people with "growth" mindsets believe that effort and persistent study trump heredity and environment, which means growth is possible for anyone. Believers in the growth mindset subscribe to "learning goals" rather than "performance goals," because the former are mastery oriented and connected to the central notion of continual development (Dweck, 2006).

Key to the idea of mastery is that we, in encouraging and support-ing it, help teachers see how they can look toward their own long-term learning journey in a series of short, success-focused development goals. Long-term development must be broken down into this kind of series so individuals can find their way through the process of development and so they can maintain the intrinsic drive for the lengthy road (Ful-lan, 2007). We hope it occurs to you that this same sort of incremental growth from an individual's starting point is at the core of differentiating instruction for students as well.

Reflect and Assess: At this point, take a moment to reflect on your own beliefs about the idea of a growth mindset and the degree to which your leadership strategies signal to teachers your unwavering belief in their capacity to grow as educators. While sifting through these ideas and questions, consider completing the following leader-ship exercise. First, think of one major initiative that has been advo-cated in your school or district. Then, think of two individual teachers who have been intimately involved with the initiative. How have their intrinsic motivators of autonomy, purpose, and mastery been sup-ported and developed through the initiative? Complete a simple com-parison chart for these two teachers and use it to reflect on what actions motivate people to sustain change over time. What does this exercise tell you about their ability to develop autonomy, purpose, and mastery?

How Does Motivation "Play Out" over the Life Span of the Differentiation Work?

The complexity of human motivation requires us to attend to teachers' individual development when designing a master plan for differentiation—a classroom practice that, itself, asks teachers to understand the complexity of student differences in order to deliver more effective instruction. In a completely rational world, just announcing a differentiation initiative and laying the proper groundwork might be enough. We all know that change does not happen that easily. In keeping with the initial idea in this chapter, it's crucial that anyone hoping to lead the implementation of responsive classroom instruction pay attention to how individuals are experiencing that change.

It is also the case that human motivation manifests itself differently over the life span of an initiative (Fullan, 2007; Huberman & Miles, 1984). In other words, individuals will respond in different ways, both emotionally and behaviorally, as they begin to understand the change, get deeper into it, and work to ensure its lasting continuation (Hall & Hord, 2001). To understand how individual motivation "plays out" over the life span of a movement to toward schoolwide differentiation, it's important to think about what goes on throughout its three phases: **initiation**, **implementation**, and **institutionalization** (Fullan, 2007).

First Phase: Initiation

Initiation is the "process that leads up to and includes a decision to adopt or proceed with a change" (Fullan, 2007, p. 69). In our experience, the initiation phase can range from a few weeks to several months.

The impetus for the change can occur along a broad range of variables. It may come from the central office, it may come as a single decision by a school leader, or it may occur after a long period of study, data analysis, and contemplation by one or multiple parties. In any case, it is essential for a leader embarking on a second-order change to lead from a compelling vision that can serve as a catalyst for teachers. They must want to share in the vision, both as an abstract idea and by taking concrete action in the classroom.

Linking vision and action is particularly important during the initiation phase of change. During this time, it's critical for teachers and other key stakeholders to have access to information about the change so that a shared understanding begins to develop. A sound communication flow between leader and colleagues is also critical during this early stage of change (Fullan, 2007). Additional factors of importance during an initiation phase relate to the scope of the initiative, time lines involved, and initial expectations for all involved. This period is also a time to assess who the best advocates may be for the process.

Dilemmas about the initiation phase are multiple and relate directly to the principles of motivation discussed earlier in this chapter. For so many initiatives, including a move to differentiated instruction, the "decision point" can feel too brief and technical. It often seems that the decision rests squarely on one person's shoulders, and only on rare occasions is that a good thing. Often, access to information and the development of advocacy are minimal or, in fact, absent. People are generally expected to "get on board" because the decision was deemed important by someone in charge—a school leader who considers his or her decision reason enough to begin the work. As Fullan (2007) reminds us, in many ways it matters less who initiates the change and more how people come to feel about the decision and its future prospects in this important first phase of change.

The principles of motivation—autonomy, purpose, and mastery—apply in the initiation phase of the work as in subsequent phases. Consideration must be given to how teachers will access the information surrounding the needed change. This data access is important—not only to establish the overall moral drive (*purpose*) for the change but also to support the teacher's need to gain information about this purpose (supporting his or her *autonomy*). In addition, at this phase of the change process, staff members will want to know how this change will unfold, particularly in terms of first steps. Indeed, some of the teachers' most immediate questions are likely to be, "What will this change look like as we begin it?" and "How will this affect me?" These are critical questions that we must be able to answer. Finally, during initiation, it is imperative that a significant number of staff members experience success with these "first steps" toward greater competence—in this case, with implementation of differentiation. This establishes a sense of beginning *mastery* and, thus, the intrinsic motivation to continue developing deeper artistry with differentiation.

Initiation Planning Checklist

❏ Is this the right time for movement toward schoolwide differentiation?
❏ Do people know the purpose of moving toward schoolwide differentiation? Is there a vision that inspires consideration of and commitment to the change?
❏ Who is supporting the change and in what ways?

❏ How widespread is the support for the change?

❏ How strategic is communication about the change toward broad implementation of differentiation? How often and how clear is the communication?

❏ In what ways will teachers have access to information about differentiation, its meaning, expectations for them, and support for the journey?

❏ How will it look when they begin to work in a more concentrated manner with differentiation in their classrooms?

Second Phase: Implementation

Implementation is putting the plan into action, and it includes all of the first steps in getting the initiative under way as well as the ongoing, thoughtful adjustments required to keep everyone moving forward. Generally speaking, it takes years for "stable" implementation and predictable results to be evident (Fullan, 2007). This does not mean that we shouldn't expect to see progress and results; we absolutely should. But the shift from learning and talking about the initiative to actually "doing it" in its intended form is a lengthy and gradual one.

At first, the implementers of the initiative (teachers) will attempt to use differentiation in any way that "seems right" to them. This experimentation is predictable and, in fact, *desirable*, in that it signals that they are making the attempt to differentiate. One of the dangers, however, is that the implementation effort will stall at this level of unsophisticated, sporadic practice. It's a situation that happens when leaders—excited to see some movement—overpraise early efforts as though those efforts equate to realization of the long-term goals. During implementation, it is important for leaders to continue to help teachers build their understanding of what *fully implemented differentiation* looks like, grasp where they are individually in that progression, and access the kind of support that will help them develop necessary competencies.

What specifically motivated each teacher to consider the change during the initiation stage may not be as compelling now. Although it is vital for leaders to continue to stress the *purpose* of the change (critically important during the initiation stage) and to encourage teachers to take risks and be experimental (supporting the *autonomy* of teachers), now the critical work is to support the idea of steady work and progress toward *mastery*.

With these three motivational factors still in play for staff and teachers, the idea of mastery will begin to take hold during implementation

as a consistent, sequential progression of skill development in differentiation, accomplished through a combination of personal mindset and
effort. What people believe about their ability to differentiate effectively
actually makes a difference in their motivation and achievement; the
extent to which teachers develop competence with and confidence in
their changing practices and see benefits for their students will alter
their behaviors in positive ways (Tschannen-Moran, 2004). Therefore,
throughout implementation, it is important to focus first on experimentation, trial and error, and supporting teachers as they make small
changes in their practices, and then concentrate on encouraging teachers to make larger changes based on the successes they have had.

Implementation is the phase when the actual work gets hard, and
we know that if teachers do not experience small successes, they may
abandon the change. Everyone has heard of teachers and schools giving up on differentiation because it's "too difficult." Again, the way to
counter this perception is to give teachers parameters and expectations
for implementation and allow them to make some choices within these
parameters (autonomy). During implementation, the work may seem
"messy," and teachers may find that it is hard to manage the changes and
incorporate them within their own practices. It will be even more important for leaders to champion the changes and the underlying purpose for
the changes. There are four dimensions that influence the implementation of any change initiative (see Figure 2.3), primarily due to how they
affect individual motivation—autonomy in particular (Fullan, 2007).

The following questions should help illuminate how the four dimensions identified can affect the rate and outcome of a differentiation
change initiative.

- **Clarity of the initiative.** How well can teachers describe the essential features of differentiation and how to implement it? Do faculty and
staff understand and share a common definition of differentiation? Do
they have an evolving understanding of what quality implementation
might look like?
- **Perceived individual need for the change.** How well do the goals
of differentiation fit with individual teachers and their prioritized needs?
- **Complexity of the change.** How difficult is the extent of the change,
and can individuals see how they can make progress with differentiation
in their own classrooms?
- **Quality and practicality of the change.** Are faculty aware of
how successful differentiation is likely to benefit their students and

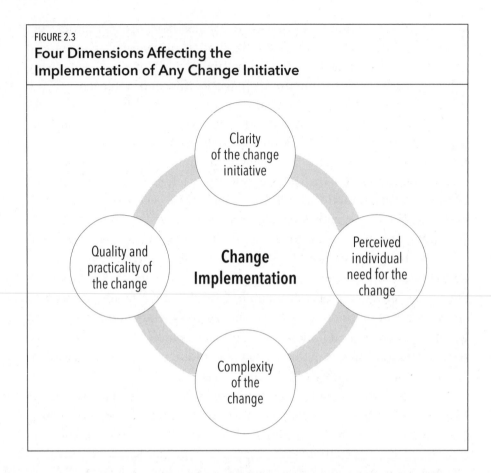

FIGURE 2.3
Four Dimensions Affecting the Implementation of Any Change Initiative

themselves, and do they see how they will get the support they need to grow in proficiency with differentiation?

The implementation phase is where changes begin to be put into play in classrooms. It is critical for us to have a thorough plan to support the development of teachers as their understanding and application of differentiation evolve. It is just as important to be flexible in the plans and to learn from each aspect of implementation in order to make the changes in leader behaviors and professional growth plans that will best support teachers as they develop their practice.

To determine "how implementation is proceeding," it is helpful to meet informally and regularly with individual teachers and staff members and engage in brief conversations about the principles and practices of differentiation in order to gain insight into their perspectives. Here are some questions to guide such conversations:

• Is the purpose of differentiation clear to you?

• How do you know there is a need for differentiation in your class(es)?

• How complex does differentiation seem to you? What have you done to make it more attainable for you?

• What motivates you to continue developing your skills in differentiating instruction?

• What should we be doing differently to support your growth in differentiating?

The answers to these questions can give valuable insight into how implementation is progressing and show if there is a need to further address the need for the change (*purpose*), break down the complexity of the change (leading to *mastery* of small first steps), and scaffold the quality and practicality of the change through additional administrative or structural supports so the implementation process results in fewer hurdles for teachers.

Implementation Planning Checklist

❏ Is there enough time to fully implement aspects of differentiation in a stepwise fashion?

❏ Is there system support for the time required to fully implement the changes?

❏ Is there a tolerance for "experimentation" with differentiation?

❏ Is there a strategic plan for regular communication and reiteration of the purpose of differentiation?

❏ Are "short-term" successes with differentiation being celebrated?

❏ Are management issues with differentiation being addressed and supported?

❏ Is there clarity about indicators of quality differentiation?

❏ Are expected changes in planning and using differentiation being broken down into manageable "chunks"?

❏ Is professional development changing to support teachers' changing needs in implementing differentiation?

Third Phase: Institutionalization

Call it routinization, incorporation, or continuation, **institutionalization** is the phase when the changes get incorporated into the school's system of practices (Fullan, 2007). Its goal is to turn improvements into routines that will outlast the presence of the leader (Sergiovanni, 1992). We like to say that institutionalization is when the change is not called anything anymore. Think about it—as long as we are calling our major work "trying to get differentiated instruction in our classrooms," we really have not institutionalized the change into practice. The mere fact that we are still naming the change signals that we are still trying to fully implement it.

During institutionalization, the change will either become part of the fabric of the school's practices or be discarded because of ineffective implementation or competing initiatives. As with the other two phases of change, there are important factors for leaders to consider at this point. Even though people have experienced some success with the differentiation, they are still attempting to fully incorporate the changes into their practice. Although the motivational factors of autonomy, purpose, and mastery still apply, specific language and type of support must change. For instance, our language now shifts into the overall purpose of incorporation and how differentiation is intended to become a part of each teacher's system of practices. During this phase, we are now encouraging teachers to extend the scope and quality of their practices and to make teaching decisions by looking at student needs and results instead of more mechanically and superficially "differentiating." During institutionalization, individual teachers must be encouraged to critically examine their practices to see how these can be deepened, strengthened, and extended.

We must remember that even during full institutionalization, the work is not "over" because we have achieved "it." We have to continue to assess results and actively develop communities of thinkers around differentiation. Further, teachers will continue to need regular encouragement, feedback, and personally relevant professional development that will make differentiation fully "theirs" so that they will embed it in daily practices and continue to refine those practices from semester to semester and year to year.

Institutionalization Planning Checklist

❑ Are people still referring to differentiation as "something we are trying to do"?

❑ How has professional development changed to show people how to deepen their practice of differentiation, focus on quality, and get even better results?

❑ Is there still regular communication about differentiation and problem solving around the use of its principles and practices?

❑ Have conditions in the school changed in ways that would impact differentiation? If so, what do these conditions demand from leaders and teachers so they can continue to grow in the practice of quality differentiation?

❑ How are teachers and teams being supported to make differentiation a permanent and increasingly productive approach to classroom practice?

Connecting the Dots: Motivation and the Phases of Planned Change

Individual development—or the cultivation of teacher growth—is an evolving practice; it looks different at the different phases of planned change. If we are savvy enough to acknowledge that idea, then we can look at motivation within the context of the life span of the change, be more strategic in growing teachers, and have a much better chance of long-lasting success.

To drive the lengthy change process and contribute to the motivational factor of purpose, leaders must develop an overall vision for the differentiation initiative. This vision will answer the question, "What are the changes we are expecting from differentiation as we progress, and how will our school look when differentiation is fully in place?" Once created, this vision for differentiation gives clarity and guidance to teachers (assisting in the motivational process) and also provides a way to evaluate the work being undertaken in support of the initiative. We'll examine the development of this kind of initiative-specific, collaborative visioning process more fully in the next chapter.

During initiation, there will likely be an almost tangible amount of energy and enthusiasm for the change and high hopes that learning to differentiate will benefit students. Cultivating autonomy, purpose, and mastery at the initiation phase requires deliberate actions by school leaders to sustain this energy as teachers take their first steps. During the early stages of implementation, however, there may be a "dip" in enthusiasm and in actual practice, as individuals face the actual challenge of changing their behaviors in classrooms and incorporating the changes into their perceptions of "full days and jammed schedules." In other words, the work of actually implementing the changes can get complicated and troublesome as teachers experiment with alterations in their practice and simultaneously realize that the change is both complex and demanding. This dip can be profound and dangerous, and if it's not addressed, the motivation to continue the work may evaporate.

Figure 2.4 spotlights the "implementation dip" (Fullan, 2007) at the end of initiation and the beginning of implementation. We will address the dip in performance in Chapter 7 and provide guidance on developing strategies to manage it and other problems of reluctance and resistance. However, it is important to note here that the implementation dip is to be expected; it's a natural part of the movement toward substantive and meaningful change resulting in responsive teaching for each learner.

FIGURE 2.4
Three Phases of the Life Span of Change

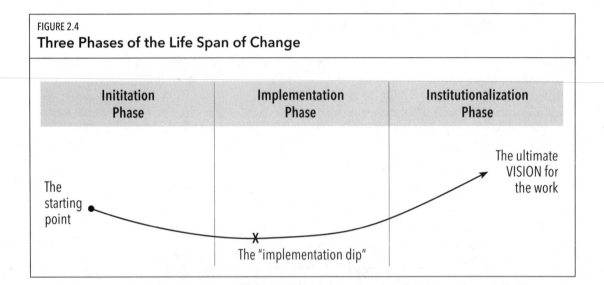

Developmentally, then, school leaders must begin to differentiate their support of teachers during implementation, addressing the clusters of individual issues that will pop up during this phase. What motivates teachers to learn about and consider change toward differentiation during initiation is not the same set of motivators that drives them during the hard work of implementation!

Reflect on these ideas as you consider this real-life example from our field experience in guiding whole-school differentiation through its phases.

Unintentional Isolation at Culver Middle School

Several years ago, as part of her regular discussions with her leadership team, Shirley Russell, the principal of Culver Junior High School, began discussing the idea of interdisciplinary teams and a move to a more authentic middle school approach. Ms. Russell also wanted these new teams to plan together to develop more differentiated approaches to addressing the needs of the school's diverse students. Her leadership team conveyed general enthusiasm for the change, and she, sensing an urgency to improve the quality of teaching, learning, and interdisciplinary collaboration, jumped at the chance to make it happen.

Prior to this, Culver was a traditional junior high school, with 55-minute class periods and an overall feel that reminded a visitor of a "mini-high school." By most observable measures, it had functioned well. Its academic departments met regularly to discuss curriculum and instructional approaches as well as to troubleshoot observed difficulties in scheduling and learning. Trust and congeniality seemed high both within and among departments at Culver, and faculty members enjoyed friendly professional and personal relationships.

The district office fully supported Ms. Russell's proposed changes and worked with the community to both reassure them and marshal community support for a name change to Culver Middle School. District officials regularly checked in with the principal to get a sense of how the changes were progressing. The district superintendent made frequent visits to the school during the initial change to offer support.

Ms. Russell and her team thought the move to interdisciplinary teams and related work with differentiated practices would go smoothly, and they planned and implemented professional development training to initiate the changes. Ms. Russell sought opportunities to consistently communicate the purpose for the change with the staff, and those opportunities seemed to go well, with little apparent opposition. New interdisciplinary teams were formed, and Ms. Russell was purposeful in linking interdisciplinary teams with differentiated instruction.

After the initial training and formation of new teams, however, Ms. Russell and her administrative team noticed there were inconsistencies in the various teams' approaches, unevenness in the way the teams were functioning, and different emphases in the discussions conducted during team meeting times. In addition, her push for teachers to begin incorporating "low-prep" differentiated teaching techniques such as exit tickets, small-group instruction, and choices of working arrangements was met with inconsistent results and varying degrees of enthusiasm. Some teachers began to openly voice resentment about their lack of involvement in the original decision to move toward differentiation and about the expectations of this new instructional approach. Old relationships suffered, and new ones among the teachers on the emerging interdisciplinary teams were slow to solidify. Some team planning times were frequently marked by open conflict, and others by brief, perfunctory meetings with superficial planning. The conversation about differentiated instruction stalled with superficial practices. Teachers began to close their doors to each other, and teacher "isolationism" became the norm as things continued to erode.

Today, a few years after the initiation of change, Culver appears to be stagnant and suffering. Although there are still interdisciplinary teams, a middle school structure, talk about differentiated instruction, and a "norm of civility" in the school, real innovation is rare and isolated. Ms. Russell hasn't seen a significant improvement in the quality of teaching and learning at the school; indeed, the detrimental effects the change has had on collaboration are confusing to her. The original idea of interdisciplinary teaming with differentiated practices—such a noble idea—is hard to find and observe.

Consider these questions as you ponder the Culver Middle School dilemma:

1. How would you describe the phases of the planned change toward interdisciplinary teams and differentiation (initiation, implementation, institutionalization)?

2. To what degree was the change understood? Was there too much at once? Why do you think so?

3. Is Culver experiencing an "implementation dip" in enthusiasm and performance? What contributed to it?

4. How did the principal build on the three motivational factors in leading the change?

5. Can Culver be extricated from this mess? How? What needs to happen to continue their efforts toward successful implementation of interdisciplinary teams and differentiated instruction?

6. What are the "leadership lessons" to be learned from this case study?

Why Care About These Ideas as You Cultivate Teacher Growth?

Our experience with Culver Middle School was complicated. Although there were certainly compelling reasons for a change toward interdisciplinary teams and differentiation, we wonder if there was clarity about the purpose of the changes across the faculty. Did the faculty clearly understand the need for interdisciplinary teams, or differentiated instruction, or both? Ms. Russell saw formation of the interdisciplinary teams as a vehicle for conversations about differentiated instruction and a way for teachers to know the Culver students better. The message may have been lost somewhere along the way to the structural, interdisciplinary team decisions. In addition, training kicked off the changes, but there was no strategic evidence of support for teachers to implement small changes leading to mastery. As is too often the case, the "announcement" of the change signaled the only apparent work to support teachers in understanding and seeing potential value in the sizeable adaptation they were being asked to make. Consequently, both the results and the relationships at Culver Middle School suffered.

We believe there is a clear pathway for incorporating the principles of rich relationships and a constant focus on results into our work to grow teachers so they can grow students. As leaders, we must pay attention to the individuals within the schools—how they relate to and work with us, how they collaborate with one other, and how they are coming to understand a change like differentiation. Working *with* teachers instead of *on* them involves a series of flexible efforts to develop and support their intrinsic motivation for personal learning and development. In this way, teachers come to establish their own goals rather than focusing solely or even largely on external demands for performance.

Dweck (2006) reminds us that the goal of leaders who want to effect significant change is to create a shared, laserlike focus on "learning at all costs" rather than causing or enabling colleagues to avoid the inevitable discomfort of uncertainty by investing their efforts in "looking smart." Using the ideas in this chapter is fundamental to growing and supporting teachers so they deeply value hard work, effort, the realization of potential, and the embracing of both challenges and obstacles as they proceed along the path of full implementation. To properly "till the soil" so that individual development can take root, we must regularly talk about the work and the struggles that will be encountered along the way. We must talk about how change will look different and feel different along the way to institutionalization. We must talk about what "drives" the group and individuals within the group.

We recommend that you, as a school leader who wants to lead a differentiation initiative, complete the "readiness chart" in Figure 2.5 as a broad assessment of whether or not your school or district is ready for

FIGURE 2.5

Readiness Chart for Long-Term Change

Download

Are These Factors Present?	If Not, What Needs to Happen?
There is a premium on building relationships with leadership and among teachers to accomplish the tasks at hand.	
The leadership exercises a "shove and a hug" philosophy, focusing on the work and results while supporting the individual development and accomplishment of teachers.	
Daily interactions support the autonomy and decision making of teachers.	
Communication and dialogue explore the purpose of the major initiatives. Teachers can clearly articulate why we are doing what we do.	
All of the major initiatives start carefully and lay out how teachers can get started with simple "first steps."	
There are thoughtful plans for the initiation portion of our work so it starts well.	
We know that implementation of the major initiatives takes time, and we clearly define each yearly change plan so people know what they are shooting for.	
Professional development continues throughout the implementation phase of the work, because we know that teachers will need additional support as they are trying to implement the practices.	
There have been dips in implementation before, but there is strategic support to minimize the length of the dips and their distractions from the vision.	
The emphasis is on constant learning and doing, instead of performance goals.	
There is a spirit of "can do" here because we have experienced full implementation before.	

this or any large-scale change initiative. The completion of this readiness chart will also provide insight on what initiation actions you need to support or modify. Carefully consider each of the factors presented. If you find any of them weak or absent in your environment, you may want to act on what needs to happen to create the conditions and environment necessary to support a focused, deliberate change to differentiated instruction or any other large-scale school or district change.

This chapter details the ingredients for leading and managing big changes in schools. The development of differentiated instruction in schools marks a change in the system of the way we "do school," so it certainly qualifies as a big and important change—a second-order change. We might assume that, as leaders, we already know a great deal about change, what motivates people to change, and how to think about change over the long term so it will last. So why do so many change efforts flounder and fail? The problem would seem to be that, too often, leaders don't act on or use what they know. Put another way, a commitment to these ideas is only a partial victory. Commitment coupled with demonstrated, regular actions signify promise that your efforts to grow differentiated practice might be successful for the long term.

Cultivating Leadership Competencies

Think about your status with the following concepts as you develop your efforts to implement differentiation. Which of the principles listed will be fodder for further self-reflection and work? Which suggest a need for continued growth of your own knowledge or skill? How might you use these principles to drive methodical, effective leadership practices to support large-scale and long-term change?

❑ I understand the power of both relationships and results in rolling out big changes such as effective differentiation.

❑ My daily leadership conversations and actions simultaneously build relationships while focusing clearly on results we need and expect from implementing differentiation.

❑ I work with individuals using what we know about what motivates people for the long term in order to support their growth with differentiation.

❑ The teachers I lead could easily describe their own sense of autonomy, purpose, and efforts toward mastery in our initiative for differentiation.

❑ I have plotted "where we are" in the life span of all of the major changes in my school or district—including movement toward effective differentiation—and I use this awareness to anticipate factors that must be considered for a particular stage of the change initiative.

❑ My teachers know "where we are" in the life span of our major changes, including differentiation, and can describe it to me and others.

❑ I have taken the "implementation pulse" so many times that my teachers anticipate these conversations. They are aware of how I use this information to adjust my leadership support for differentiation.

Download

3

Designing a Vision for the Differentiated Landscape

Recall that purpose, or vision, helps motivate people to initiate and implement the work of school improvement. Vision is absolutely the right place for leaders to begin leading for differentiation. Recall, too, that leading for differentiation is fluid. The support for and development of teachers has to change over time as they move from starting the work to being in the thick of it. In this chapter, we examine an overarching strategy for creating the kind of differentiation you want to see in your school. That key strategy is developing an *operational vision*. As the terms suggests, the strategy's goal is to turn a somewhat abstract idea into concrete and actionable terms. Characterized by specificity and clarity about how the work will progress, an operational vision should not only motivate people to initiate change toward differentiation but also help guide and sustain their work over the years.

How Do Schools Commonly Plan for the Work Ahead?

Before we explore the content of an operational vision, why it's necessary, and how to design one for a differentiated school, let's pause to think about the process of visioning and planning that is probably most common in schools and in districts. The following scenario might look familiar to you.

A Noble (If Futile) Yearly Process

It's one week before the first day of a new school year, and the folks at Hewitt High School gather for a predictable—and district-required—yearly exercise: a series of meetings in which they brainstorm or review the school's vision and mission. Faculty members are asked to "imagine what the school needs to look like" in the future and boil down this vision into a list of lofty ideas. Then, as a second act to this school play, they are asked to create a "bumper sticker" or slogan-like statement to express the work that they do. This, it's explained, is the school's mission statement.

This year, as every year, Hewitt teachers generally participate willingly, if not particularly enthusiastically, in these exercises. This year, as every year, the vision and the mission statement they come up with will be blown up into poster-size displays and placed prominently in the school entrance. And this year, as every year, within a few days, these displays will fade into the background. Teachers will scarcely notice them, let alone use them to reflect on their own practices. The official vision and mission will be essentially forgotten until next year, when the Hewitt faculty will gather, as required, and go through the same process all over again.

For many of us, this "noble process" has a familiar ring, and, for years, we (Carol and Mike) have participated in the creation of vision statements and mission statements with schools and districts. And despite the good intentions behind these sessions, and the earnest efforts of everyone involved, most of the statements generated wound up gathering dust rather than driving people to create meaningful changes in their schools. We suspect that the creation of a vision and mission has become perfunctory. In this chapter, we'll suggest ways to turn a vision for differentiation into an effective driver of change. First, however, let's examine a key problem with creating visions and missions: confusion over terminology. Figure 3.1 presents three key definitions we will use in offering guidance for planning schoolwide movement toward differentiation: **vision**, **operational vision**, and **yearly change plans**. These are separate but tightly interconnected elements in change planning and management. Vision is about the principles, practices, moral imperatives, and potentials that propel the work of the leader and staff, and the operational vision is the "word picture" that describes the desired

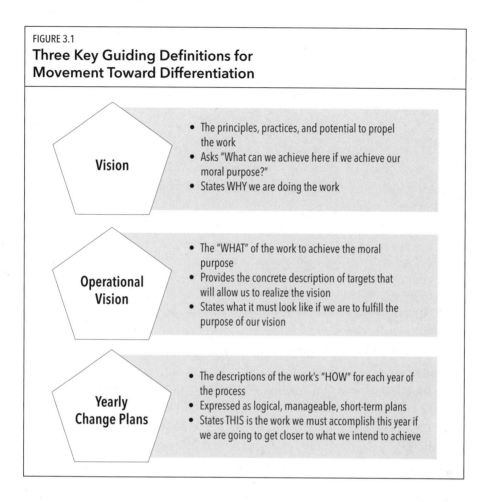

FIGURE 3.1
Three Key Guiding Definitions for Movement Toward Differentiation

Vision
- The principles, practices, and potential to propel the work
- Asks "What can we achieve here if we achieve our moral purpose?"
- States WHY we are doing the work

Operational Vision
- The "WHAT" of the work to achieve the moral purpose
- Provides the concrete description of targets that will allow us to realize the vision
- States what it must look like if we are to fulfill the purpose of our vision

Yearly Change Plans
- The descriptions of the work's "HOW" for each year of the process
- Expressed as logical, manageable, short-term plans
- States THIS is the work we must accomplish this year if we are going to get closer to what we intend to achieve

future. It's the translation of what we ultimately desire into concrete terms or targets. Finally, yearly change plans describe the "mission" of every year: the actions we must take to continue moving closer to our vision and the operational vision.

Power Shift: Why Have an Operational Vision for Differentiation?

An easily understood definition of a **vision** is "a realistic, credible, attractive future for the organization" (DuFour, DuFour, & Eaker, 2008, p. 472). Because we have found that a compelling vision is a powerful driver in school change, we will emphasize the importance of a specific vision in the journey toward differentiation. Refer to Chapter 1 for a discussion of some possible visions for differentiation.

Every leader should think deeply and broadly about a vision before attempting to lead from it. A worthy vision will necessarily stay in the foreground of conversation and will do so indefinitely. Although such a vision should capture the attention and interest of all stakeholders in a school, on its own, it won't change anything. For that reason, it's critical that we as leaders engage our colleagues in creating a word picture of what everyone who is part of the school faculty and staff will need to do to translate the vision's idea into everyday action. We will call this action-oriented document an **operational vision**. There are several standards for this sort of operational vision (adapted from DuFour et al., 2008)—criteria that are essential to support its successful development and communication. In short, the operational vision for schoolwide differentiation must do the following:

• Clearly convey what differentiated instruction will look like.

• Appeal to the long-term interests of the people who work in the school.

• Be realistic but challenging to people who will implement the changes.

• Be focused and clear enough to provide guidance in decision making and evaluation of progress.

• Be flexible enough to allow for some autonomy and individual responses in light of changing conditions in the school.

• Support communication and explanation to stakeholders.

Traditionally, school leaders have facilitated a vision-casting process for the school as a whole: *This is what we want our school to be like and look like.* (Remember the example of Hewitt High School.) Although it is important for a school's staff to have this overall sense of what excellence looks like in their school, we often find that staffs who are attempting to move toward differentiation have not described what excellence looks like for differentiation *specifically*. As a result, they don't have an agreed-upon definition of differentiation or sets of markers that will help them move toward quality differentiation. It may indeed be useful to have an overall, more generic school or district vision statement, but when engaging in fundamental change, it is more important to have a specific operational vision for what the new practices look like, articulated by the major stakeholders who will be affected.

🛠 *Dig Deep:* Think about the vision statement you have for your school or work. Then consider whether or not you have worked with others to define a vision for differentiation as you ask yourself these questions:

- How useful would an operational vision for differentiation be?
- How could it become a powerful communication tool for you?
- How could teachers use such a vision to assess their own progress toward differentiation?

When school staffs have an operational word picture of what it will eventually look like when deep, sophisticated differentiated instruction is in place in all classrooms, they know what to aim for. As leaders, we can use the operational vision to guide individual conversations with teachers, encouraging them to use it as a basis for comparison as they examine their own knowledge, skills, and practice and set goals for their personal development and growth. We have already suggested that purpose, a key motivational element (Pink, 2009), helps move people toward a vision to initiate change. Figure 3.2 shows how the type of operational vision we propose here supports the three fundamental motivational principles briefly explored in Chapter 2.

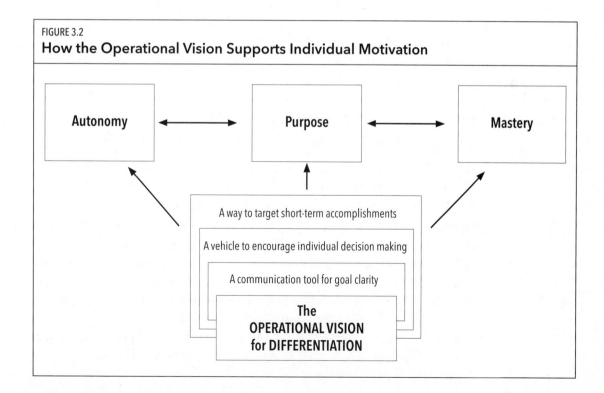

FIGURE 3.2
How the Operational Vision Supports Individual Motivation

Autonomy ⟷ Purpose ⟷ Mastery

A way to target short-term accomplishments

A vehicle to encourage individual decision making

A communication tool for goal clarity

The
**OPERATIONAL VISION
for DIFFERENTIATION**

Having a clear vision for differentiation allows everyone engaged in the change effort to participate in conversations about the purpose of the work, the "big why" that can often motivate and satisfy people to "hitch their desires to a cause larger than themselves" (Pink, 2009, p. 131), but having an operational vision for differentiation is what formally establishes it as a key school priority and helps teachers align its elements with other work they see as critical to their success. Engaging teachers in developing the operational vision and in ongoing conversations about its significance contributes to autonomy. It gives them more voice and choice in how things proceed—and ownership of differentiation's success.

The operational vision holds additional power for school leaders and leadership teams. We are obligated to evaluate progress toward differentiation, and the operational vision sets the "ultimate destination" against which school staffs can benchmark. Teachers too can see where their short-term wins are in relation to the larger destination. This sense of ongoing progress toward mastery contributes to and reinforces a growth mindset. In sum, a clearly defined and focused effort for differentiated classrooms holds tremendous promise as a strategy for creating more responsive classrooms and achieving real student growth. Because an operational vision serves as a compass for long-term teacher growth toward this goal and for leadership support along the way, it's key to the successful forward progress of effective schoolwide differentiation. See Figure 3.3 for a summary of the power of an operational vision for differentiation.

How Do We Prepare School Staffs to Create an Operational Vision for Differentiation?

Before teachers and leaders can talk about an operational vision for differentiation, they need to have foundational understanding of differentiated practices and a simple set of constructs for the discussions to come. In readying everyone to develop an operational vision for differentiation, we believe an organic approach is generally the best one. To us, "organic" means that the understanding of differentiation is allowed to grow and develop through learning, trial, and error before the vision is created. That may sound counterintuitive, but it really isn't. The more powerful visions for differentiation emerge *after* people have had some experiences with differentiated practices. In effect, they feel more comfortable planning for differentiation because they have some working knowledge of it.

FIGURE 3.3

The Power of an Operational Vision for Differentiation

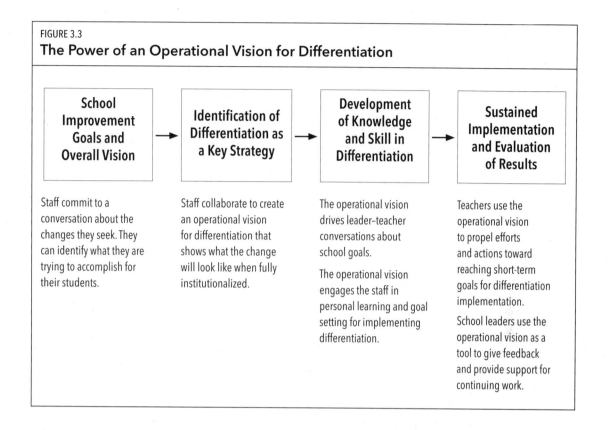

School Improvement Goals and Overall Vision	Identification of Differentiation as a Key Strategy	Development of Knowledge and Skill in Differentiation	Sustained Implementation and Evaluation of Results
Staff commit to a conversation about the changes they seek. They can identify what they are trying to accomplish for their students.	Staff collaborate to create an operational vision for differentiation that shows what the change will look like when fully institutionalized.	The operational vision drives leader–teacher conversations about school goals. The operational vision engages the staff in personal learning and goal setting for implementing differentiation.	Teachers use the operational vision to propel efforts and actions toward reaching short-term goals for differentiation implementation. School leaders use the operational vision as a tool to give feedback and provide support for continuing work.

Based on this assumption, readiness to create an operational vision for differentiation involves a few key facets. We recommend that leaders employ three practices to prepare staff members to create an informed and galvanizing operational vision for the work ahead.

Storytelling. First, we must engage school staff in a conversation about "how we got here," involving the teachers in discussions about the critical problems and needs the school is facing and why differentiated practices can accelerate their progress toward their ultimate purpose. This storytelling helps make the case that the vision is worthy of people's consideration and, ultimately, worthy of their commitment. In practical terms, this storytelling may involve team data analysis; informal conversations with individual teachers; and key conversations in leadership teams, with department chairs, and with grade-level chairs. Storytelling sets the stage for teachers and staff members to reflect on successes, needs, and the future. We can engage teachers and staff members in storytelling over a period of time to prepare them for the visioning process.

Professional Development 101. A second key aspect of preparation for the visioning process involves professional learning—in this case, a focus on the fundamentals of differentiation. Usually delivered as whole-faculty training, this foundational professional development aims at helping teachers acquire knowledge and establish a common understanding of the possibilities of differentiated instruction. At the outset, there will be more emphasis on "what differentiation is and isn't" (see Figure 3.4) than pressure to implement practices. The goal of this phase of learning is to create a baseline of shared understanding and to spark reflection and speculation about how differentiation can affect teachers and students in positive ways.

Checking on Worries. A third key in preparation to create an operational vision for differentiation is to acknowledge that this change may cause anxiety, worries, and even illogical emotional reactions. We believe that during this preparatory stage, school leaders and teacher leaders must engage in transparent conversations regarding concerns individuals have about the anticipated change. Believe it or not, these conversations will actually build trust in us as leaders; they communicate that emotional reactions to the work are natural, valued, and respected. We'll share additional thoughts about understanding and addressing staff concerns in Chapter 4, and in Chapter 6, we will share a tool leaders can deploy to quickly assess worries.

What Is a Sound Process for Crafting an Operational Vision for Differentiated Classrooms?

Weighing progress with the three preparatory elements described will help determine when the time is right to begin the earnest dialogue that is key to developing an operational vision for differentiation. It is often best for this process to involve as many people as possible. By doing so, we send a clear message about ownership, collaboration, and the desire to develop a common vocabulary and dialogue around differentiated instruction.

In Figure 3.5, we present a process you can follow to guide your staff through a vision-casting meeting—the development of an operational vision for differentiation. After a few hours of work, which can occur in one extended session (as in the figure's model) or over time, the process generates a "word picture" in the minds of the school's faculty and staff, of what, differentiated instruction in the school could and *should* be. We've been very specific in this model, even suggesting time frames and

FIGURE 3.4
What Differentiation Is and Is Not

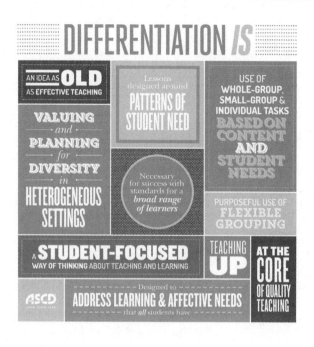

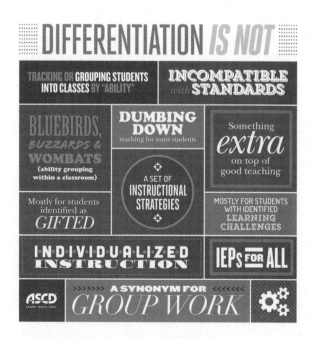

FIGURE 3.5

A Process for Launching an Operational
Vision Statement for Differentiation

Time Frame: This meeting should last about 2–2.5 hours.

Set Up: You will need tables with 4–6 chairs around each, wall space, a table for materials, and a chart stand.

Materials: Chart paper and stands, chart markers, half-sheet cardstock, large (5" x 7") index cards, tape for walls, and stickers or colored dots for "voting."

1. Establishing a Common Base of Understanding

Participants should be seated at tables in groups of 4–6 to facilitate conversation. It's important that people have an understanding of what they are about to do *before* they arrive at the meeting. You may also want to do a "warm-up" to focus the group.

Ask participants to think about and talk about the changes needed in the school's classrooms so that students will be more successful. In doing this, reflect on the school's overall vision to help them talk about their moral purpose. Encourage them to reflect on what they have learned about differentiated instruction during the professional development Ithey've received and through their experimentation with differentiation practices.

Tell them that they will be creating an operational vision for differentiation, and remind them what the operational vision can achieve for the school. Have them think about how teaching and learning will look different when differentiation is fully in place and thriving. Prompt them to think in terms of (a) what *students* are doing when supported with differentiated instruction, (b) what *teachers* are doing when practicing differentiated instruction, and (c) how the *school* is organized to support differentiated instruction. You may want to add more categories such as (d) how *parents* are involved. Have a slide or visual prepared to spur thinking.

Distribute large index cards and ask each participant to individually "idea write" for a few minutes. Ask that this be a silent activity.

2. Conducting Focused Conversation About Differentiated Teaching and Learning

Rearrange participants (ask them to take their index cards) into "focused" groups–*students*, *teachers*, or *school*–and ask each group to discuss in detail how students, teachers, or the school will be different when differentiated instruction is thriving. What will they be doing? How will they be organized? Assign a group facilitator if need be. You may have more than one table addressing each group/aspect.

Participants at each table should compare their ideas and brainstorm a table list with 5–8 "visions." These statements will just be for the group that has been given to them (students, teachers, or school). It can be helpful to have the groups write each of their 5–8 ideas on a single piece of sturdy cardstock.

As the groups work, post three sheets of chart paper, each headed with a group/aspect under discussion (e.g., *Students, Teachers,* and *School*). At the end of a set period of time, ask one person from each table to post the table's pieces of cardstock under the appropriate heading.

3. Prioritizing the Vision for Each Group/Aspect and Beginning the Drafting

Ask the entire group of participants to reconvene in one large group for this conversation. At this juncture, you may have had more than one table group address a particular component, so this time will allow for them to notice any response patterns. Engage the group in an affinity process to clarify statements and to identify and consolidate duplicate ideas.

Distribute sheets of stickers ("sticky dots") and invite all participants to approach the charts and silently "vote" for the vision statements they would most like to see realized by putting their stickers on any/all of the ideas they value the most in each of the categories.

Lead a discussion of the voting and copy the most valued statements for each group (as determined by voting) as bullet points onto a fresh sheet of chart paper, set up as shown:

> At _____ School, we are
> committed to developing and institution-
> alizing differentiated instruction, where
>
> Students are
>
> Teachers are
>
> The school is organized to

At this point, you have a draft of your operational vision statement for differentiation.

4. Confirming the New Vision for Differentiation

Ask participants to get back into their groups again and discuss the draft statement and its pros and cons. Give participants plenty of time to do this, and provide questions to deliberate. Questions may include
- Which of the statements does your group feel most passionate about?
- Which statement needs clarification?
- What did we leave out?

Ask all participants to vote on how much they can support this draft vision statement (fist to five) *or* ask each person to write a personal commitment to the vision, sign it, and use it as an exit ticket for the scheduled break.

5. Work Team Editing and Finalization

Identify 3–5 people who are willing to "edit" the draft statement for clarity of language, uniformity, and readability. These editors can be preassigned or volunteers. Ask them to edit the vision and to report back to the entire group within a predetermined time.

materials, but we invite you to adapt the process to fit your particular needs and context.

The plan for developing an organizational vision suggested here allows school staff members to draw on their beginning understanding of differentiation to operationally define what teaching and learning look like when teachers work with varied student needs in mind. In addition, the visioning process encourages stakeholders to look at the most affected groups of people or structures, such as students, teachers, and the school as a unit. Although the process is shown here in a tidy figure, its reality will be fluid and even a little messy, as collaborative approaches tend to be.

The vision-casting meeting is a perfect time for participants to take a few hours to focus on differentiated instruction, assess what they know about it, and begin to literally design what it should look like when fully institutionalized. As in any productive meeting, ideas and perspectives will be offered and explored. Leaders and participants alike should be prepared for varieties of opinions and trust the process to bring everyone to consensus. A key goal for us, as leaders, should be creating an environment that is both safe and productive—one in which colleagues can have honest discussions and still create a satisfying blueprint for action.

Let's look at a few examples of operational vision statements for differentiated instruction that demonstrate the kind of clarity and practical language that should be your aim. Note that each statement is a clear description, giving everyone who reads it an accurate image of what that element will like in practice. And consider that all the statements, when combined, do become operational in nature, detailing what effective differentiation looks like in classrooms and what priorities are most critical to those who crafted the operational vision:

We are committed to developing and institutionalizing differentiated instruction, where

Teachers are
 • Talking comfortably with students about the nature of differentiation, why it matters, and the roles each person in the class can play to ensure its effectiveness.
 • Establishing clear learning goals in terms of critical knowledge, understanding, and skill.
 • Creating daily plans, with colleagues and teams when possible, that address varied student readiness levels, interests, and approaches to learning.
 • "Teaching up" on a daily basis to establish and support high expectations for all students.
 • Using formative assessment seamlessly to gain insights about adjustments to teaching plans in order to help all students take their next steps in learning progressions.
 • Selecting instructional strategies and approaches that invite attention to learner variance while focusing on essential learning goals.
 • Developing with students classroom routines that balance flexibility and predictability.

Students are
 • Talking easily about what differentiation means, how it looks, and why it matters.

• Referring to specific learning goals in terms of knowledge, understanding, and skill.

• Moving easily into multiple grouping settings during the day to focus on appropriate tasks.

• Demonstrating an understanding of formative assessment and their personal results by setting and working toward individual learning goals.

• Assisting peers to articulate, work toward, and achieve their learning goals.

• Conversing with teachers about refining classroom routines, selecting appropriate learning tools and resources, and working in ways that support success.

The school is organized to

• Focus teachers and community in understanding differentiation by using consistent language, resources, and support for differentiation.

• Provide time for teachers to collaborate on a daily basis to design plans to meet the varied needs of students.

• Provide in-class coaching and support to help each teacher take his or her next steps in the five key components of differentiation.

• Require the use of daily formative assessments to provide information for planning and carrying out instructional plans.

• Provide feedback to teachers about their growth in effectively using the five key elements of differentiation (environment, curriculum, assessment, instruction, classroom leadership and management) to support the varied learning needs of students in their classrooms.

• Create classroom support teams of instructional specialists who work collaboratively with teachers to design and use instructional plans and materials that support the success of a broad range of learners.

Can the Operational Vision for Differentiated Instruction Be Overwhelming?

The simple answer? Yes. In fact, if we stop with the creation of an overall operational vision, we will find ourselves unable to manage effectively from that vision. As the examples we've looked at illustrate, an operational vision for differentiation is all-encompassing, large, and long-term, detailing how stakeholders will ultimately be functioning, how students will be participating, and how the school will look to support the work well into the future. Teachers may simultaneously like the process of defining the vision for differentiation in operational terms and be daunted or even frustrated by questions of how they will attain these challenging aspirations.

Another step is needed, then, before the operational vision can be unleashed as a powerful motivator and driver toward differentiation. Therefore, sometime late in the initiation stage of the change and before the majority of teachers have begun to earnestly implement differentiation principles in their classrooms, the leader and the change leadership team must revisit the newly minted operational vision to create the first **yearly change plan**. This plan is much shorter than the operational vision; it gives both leaders and teachers a way to engage in what Peter Senge (1999) calls "vision horizoning": imagining themselves at the starting point of the great initiative (in this case, differentiation) and looking across the horizon to the operational vision statement in the far future.

The operational vision might be realistically actualized only after three to five years of implementation. Thus, the leader's task here at the beginning of the implementation phase is to involve as many stakeholders as possible in describing what *this year's* success will look like. Vision horizoning makes the change journey seem shorter and more "doable" to the participating staff members, and yet, because the change plan was derived from the long-range operational vision, the yearly plans and the ultimate differentiation destination are aligned. Recall our definitions of and distinctions among vision, operational vision, and yearly change plans. The yearly change plans drive the work to achieve the operational vision, which in turn serves the larger vision of the school. The vision is the "why," the operational vision is the "what," and the yearly change plan is the "how."

As the name indicates, yearly change plans should be created every year of implementation to break down the operational vision into doable "chunks" of goals. Teachers are less likely to be overwhelmed when it's clear that they aren't expected to actualize each of the changes illustrated in the words of the operational vision all at once; they're pursuing realistic changes in practice over manageable one-year plans. The use of yearly change plans, then, supports what we know about motivation theory and about individual mastery as a motivator. See Figure 3.6 for a graphic depiction of a yearly change plan's function and how each sequential change plan relates to the ultimate outcomes.

In practical terms, we recommend using a backward design process (Wiggins & McTighe, 2005) to derive the yearly change plans from the overall operational vision; with this approach, you're assured that each

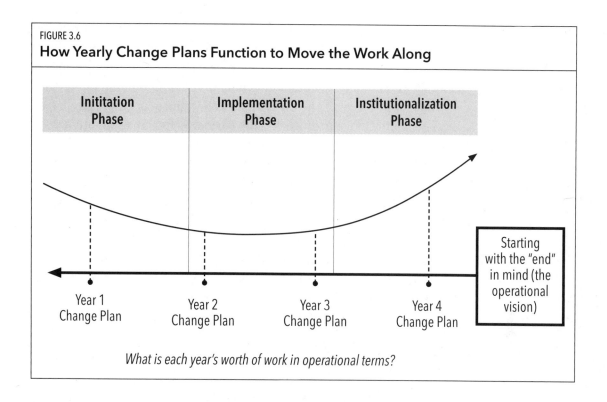

FIGURE 3.6
How Yearly Change Plans Function to Move the Work Along

| Inititation Phase | Implementation Phase | Institutionalization Phase |

Year 1 Change Plan

Year 2 Change Plan

Year 3 Change Plan

Year 4 Change Plan

Starting with the "end" in mind (the operational vision)

What is each year's worth of work in operational terms?

change plan drives the work, conversations, and evaluation of progress toward the ultimate vision for differentiation. The bottom arrow in Figure 3.6 points backward from that ultimate differentiation vision and depicts four years of yearly change plans that drive the work of the school toward that vision. Of particular note is the implementation dip (see p. 36). The creation of yearly change plans allows a school to chart specific courses of action to minimize or eliminate barriers that are preventing people from deeply implementing differentiated teaching practices.

Although the process for creating each change plan need not be as lengthy and involved as the process for creating an operational vision, it should be collaborative and promote dialogue.

Questions to Consider When Assembling the Yearly Change Plan Team

• Who was involved in the initial creating of the operational vision, and who needs to be a part of this yearly change plan process? What degree of consistency will benefit us most?

• How soon does the change plan need to be developed to keep us from losing momentum?

• How will we use the change plan to drive our conversations this year?

• How will we achieve appropriate goal uniformity and still allow teachers the autonomy to articulate and pursue their own goals?

• How will we use the change plan to provide the variety of supports necessary for teacher success with the plan?

• How can we create the change plan so it gives us clear ideas as to how to evaluate the year of work, both formatively and summatively?

The development of the yearly change plan begins by anchoring this new task to the operational vision for differentiation. Although we strongly believe that the designing of the overall operational vision should be a "flat process" where all stakeholders have their voices in the creation, we recommend that the yearly change plan process be completed in a more advisory fashion, since the leader's job is to lead the work toward differentiation and manage the yearly press toward the vision. Figure 3.7 maps out a process for conducting the change plan meeting and developing a change plan. Again, we invite you to modify this process according to what will work best in the context of your school's culture and organization.

What Do Yearly Change Plans Look Like in Action?

Yearly change plans describe what change looks like for the coming year, generally in terms of students, teachers, and school organization. Although we recommend a standard format for the overall operational vision (see Figure 3.5), we believe that yearly change plans may take a variety of formats, depending on the particular circumstances of the school.

As an example, the leaders in Tennessee's Greeneville City Schools chose to create their Year One change plan via a process very similar to the one described in Figure 3.7. But they also wanted to create a powerful visual to illustrate the change plan components—something to demonstrate the ongoing nature of the work. You can see the yearly change plan format they chose in Figure 3.8, along with the actions they decided to undertake in the first year of differentiation implementation.

The Greeneville City Schools change plan described their "theory" of how their work in differentiation would change practices and decisions during the first year of initiated work. Central to this theory was the idea that each one of their described changes could be assessed and monitored.

FIGURE 3.7

A Process for Creating a Yearly Change Plan

Time Frame: 2 hours

Set Up: You will need tables with 4–6 chairs around each table, wall space, a table for materials, and a chart stand.

Materials: Chart paper and stands, chart markers, large index cards, tape for walls, and stickers or colored dots for "voting" (if needed or desired).

1. Backward Design Reflection

Divide participants into small groups (4–6) and direct them back to the operational vision statement and the groups/structures listed there (e.g., students, teachers, principals, schools, and perhaps parents) and ask them to speculate on what has to happen the year *before* the vision is realized (e.g., if the vision is five years away, what has to happen in Year Four, Year Three, and so on). Ask them to talk in general terms about the characteristics and behaviors of each group/structure. Continue the process until they have talked and written in general terms about each year's growth in all the categories, ending the process with Year One (or the year of work closest to the present). This portion of the reflection may result in a series of chart papers, posted in a "backward fashion" beginning with the operational vision and working back to the current year, with descriptions in general about how the groups must change.

2. Change Identification

Tell the participants they will be thinking about and then writing about what changes they believe are reasonable for this year of implementation, or, in other words, what change will look like after the coming year (e.g., Year One). Ask them to think about these changes in terms of those same groups or structures represented in their overall operational vision statement (e.g., students, teachers, and school organization). Remind them that this year, they may not anticipate significant changes in some of the groups or structures, and this is perfectly acceptable. They are to think of the most significant changes for the most important groups or structures this year.

Ask each individual to now write each of his or her ideas on an index card, articulating what a year's worth of actions and changes should look like in order to be both stimulating and reasonable. At this point, participants may need some examples to help spur their thinking. For example: *Teachers begin studying assessment and the role of formative assessment in driving instruction* or *Teachers use exit/entry cards and other low-prep formative assessment strategies and use the results to alter their instructional plans.*

Allow time for individual thinking and writing until participants have generated a few ideas for all of groups/structures in the operational vision.

3. Discussion of Key Strategies

Ask all participants to then move into small groups of 4–6 (leader's choice as to how to move them). They work with each other to share their ideas and develop 5–7 key change plan strategies that detail the actions and give insights as to what "success" looks like for that year of work. A scribe from each table writes each of the table's ideas for each group or structure on a large piece of cardstock or paper, with print that's large enough to be read from a distance. At the end of a set period of time, ask someone from each table to post these ideas under the appropriate heading (students, parents, or school). *Note:* If you had 5 tables of 6 people each, you should have about 25–35 ideas posted in total somewhere under the 3 charts.

4. Examining, Prioritizing, and Discussing Possible Change Actions

Lead the participants in a discussion of the postings, weeding out duplicates, combining and clarifying action ideas, and so on. At this point, if one major heading has fewer ideas than others, lead the group in a discussion so more ideas can be generated and posted.

Ask each table to review all the assembled change actions and create their "top 10" list of the 10 most important "moves" for this year's work in differentiation. They should record their list on a piece of chart paper. When the lists are complete, post them side by side, lead a group examination for similarities, and share general thoughts and concerns. Ask each table to generate a "report to the group" that evaluates the overall suggestions for actions and highlights any questions the table has.

At this point, thank the participants for their work and describe how their suggestions will be carefully reviewed and used in crafting the change plan for the year. Upon completion, take the "top 10" lists and either summarize and create the change plan from the summary, or give the top 10 lists to your leadership team for discussion, summary, and decision at their next meeting. Your goal will be to create a change plan that succinctly illustrates "how" knowledge, skill, and implementation will look for the year, clearly communicating what the emphasis for that year will be.

FIGURE 3.8

A Sample Yearly Change Plan for the Greeneville (TN) City Schools

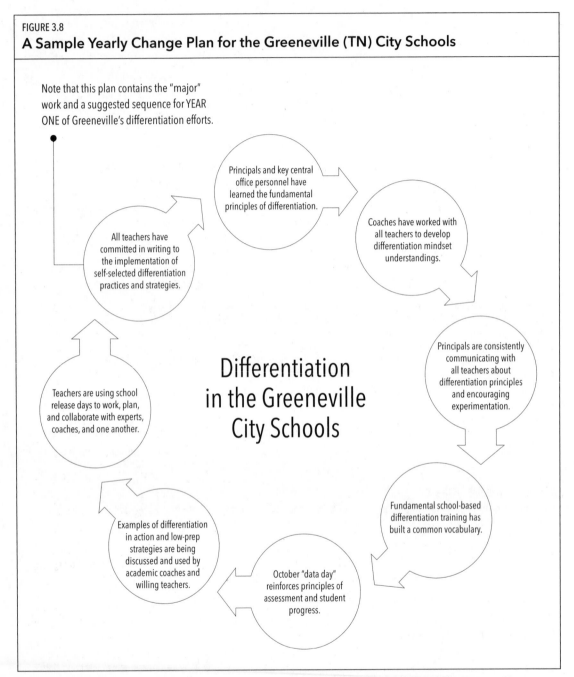

Note that this plan contains the "major" work and a suggested sequence for YEAR ONE of Greeneville's differentiation efforts.

Principals and key central office personnel have learned the fundamental principles of differentiation.

Coaches have worked with all teachers to develop differentiation mindset understandings.

Principals are consistently communicating with all teachers about differentiation principles and encouraging experimentation.

Fundamental school-based differentiation training has built a common vocabulary.

October "data day" reinforces principles of assessment and student progress.

Examples of differentiation in action and low-prep strategies are being discussed and used by academic coaches and willing teachers.

Teachers are using school release days to work, plan, and collaborate with experts, coaches, and one another.

All teachers have committed in writing to the implementation of self-selected differentiation practices and strategies.

Differentiation in the Greeneville City Schools

Source: From *Orchestrating School Change* (p. 64) by Michael Murphy, 2014, Huntington Beach, CA: Shell Education. Copyright 2014 by Shell Education. Adapted with permission.

In crafting the Greeneville City Schools plan, leaders decided that the focus of the first year would be on adults (particularly teachers) and school structural changes. To break it down further, the changes, listed for each of those "facets" of strategic work, included the following:

The Greeneville City Schools Change Plan for Year One

Teachers and Leaders	School Structures
Teachers and leaders are knowledgeable in fundamentals of differentiated instruction.	Schedules include informal times for academic coaches to work with teachers on differentiated principles.
Teachers are beginning to experiment in differentiated practices.	October "data day" focuses on formative assessment and implications of data analysis.
Teachers are implementing low-prep differentiated strategies and discussing their value in informal meetings.	Early release days are targeted for differentiation discussions and collaborative lesson planning.
Principals are using informal communication and individual conferences to promote differentiated practices.	

During the first year of Greenville City School District's differentiation implementation, principals didn't focus—or focus their teachers—on the comprehensive and potentially overwhelming overall operational vision; they focused on the Year One change plan. This practice allowed teachers to "see themselves" in differentiation—that is, to see how their thinking and classroom practices would look as they moved toward more consistent and effective differentiation—and identify what was expected of them over the first year. As it turned out, many of the district's teachers progressed well beyond the change plan goals for Year One, and, in fact, this was encouraged. Still, the Year One change plan presented the game plan for efforts and provided guidance for assessing progress in the first year of differentiation implementation.

In brief, yearly change plans provide leaders with a structure for communication about and assessment of efforts for each year, and provide teachers and staff members with guidance for the kinds of incremental and strategic changes they need to make. For each year of work toward full implementation and progress toward institutionalization, the yearly change plans focus conversation and assessment for the school leader as he or she orchestrates the plans and nurtures motivation toward the eventual vision.

How Can Yearly Change Plans Drive Conversations for Growth?

Yearly change plan conversations can be powerful if we have faith that using these plans to guide teachers' growth will help us build relationships, accomplish short-term actions, and realize results. Here's an example of a how a yearly change plan implemented by a savvy principal ignited his school's differentiation efforts.

Mountain View Intermediate School Focuses on Talk to Drive Change

A few months ago, the staff at Mountain View Intermediate School completed a process for developing an operational vision. It was the result of months of study, professional learning, and dialogue about differentiated practices and how these practices would deepen teaching and learning at their school. After some time in this initiation phase, the principal, Dr. Kurt Pederson, determined that it was time to bring the group back together to fashion a yearly change plan for the first year of experimentation, learning, and implementation of differentiated instructional practices and strategies.

The yearly change plan detailed the modifications that were expected in the first year in terms of teachers, leaders, and school structures. Dr. Pederson used this first year change plan to formulate his leadership and management plan for the second half of the year, which included the following:

• Weekly informal one-on-one conversations with teachers about their individual progress toward the change plan growth and development (scheduled so that by the end of each month, he has a sense of where most teachers are in their changes).

• Monthly communications with parents and the community, highlighting not only the vision for differentiation but also progress on the Year One change plan.

• Attention to trust and the culture of collaboration in the school to support idea sharing, including "matchmaking" of teachers who are working on similar ideas and changes.

• The use of anecdotal evaluation data such as observations and conversation logs to track growth.

• Monthly meetings with his leadership team to consider ongoing needs for structural changes the school can make to support time, resources, or collaboration among the teachers.

The vision for differentiation can be the "rallying cry" for the change. If properly handled, it can be energizing and coalescing for teachers and staff. Reflect for a minute on the major concepts of this chapter:

• The importance of an operational vision as a way of focusing differentiation targets.

• The value of defining an operational vision to drive the work, serve as a communication link, and establishing a framework for evaluation.

• The process of casting an operational vision for differentiation.

• The value of creating a yearly change plan for each of the multiple years of work toward the operational vision.

• The process of casting yearly change plans for the operational vision.

• The potential for using the operational vision and change plans on a regular basis to manage and lead your school's differentiation work.

We hope you have developed some clarity with fundamental ideas about vision and the power of vision to drive the work toward differentiated practices in schools. When developed and used in weekly conversations and management strategies, two things—an operational vision and yearly change plans—are invaluable in fashioning the best instruction possible for the ultimate stakeholders, the students we serve.

Cultivating Leadership Competencies

Think about your status with the following concepts as you develop your efforts to implement differentiation. As you consider these statements, map out a plan for enacting differentiation that incorporates these fundamental ideas. What are some of the things that need to shift in your own mindset? How could you engage and use others' expertise in developing a vision for the work?

❏ We have developed an operational vision for differentiation in our school(s).

❏ I understand and use the operational vision for multiple purposes—to spark conversations, to monitor progress, and to evaluate results.

❏ Our operational vision is connected to "yearly change plans" to drive the work forward in a manageable way.

❏ We focus on short-term "wins" so people remain motivated to achieve the vision.

 Download

4

Cultivating Deep Adult Learning

As we have seen, the initial vision for differentiation defines what everyone ultimately hopes to achieve, the operational vision paints a word picture of quality differentiated practices, and change plans create mechanisms to achieve the operational vision, year by year. These are all powerful tools for school leaders. Equally significant, though, is *how* people in the school will acquire the critical knowledge and skills they need to implement the changes described in the operational vision. The obvious answer is professional development—and yet professional development as a pathway to school improvement has something of an image problem. This reputation is often well earned. As Mike has put it, "Much of professional development seems misguided, unfocused, bloated at the beginning of an initiative, and not created or orchestrated to maintain the energy and skill needed to institutionalize the change" (Murphy, 2014, p. 93).

How Can We Make Professional Development a Key Change Element for Differentiation?

The challenge is to design and implement professional development that is actually effective. We definitely believe this is possible, but the answer does not lie in a formula or a series of steps. Instead, we suggest three guiding ideas to consider.

Idea #1: Effective Professional Development Adapts over Time

In Chapter 2, we talked about the life span of a change initiative and demonstrated how adults respond in varying ways as they get deeper into the work and are compelled to begin trying out the new changes in their classrooms. These individualized responses are often laced with emotion as well as varying perceptions of what degree of knowledge and skill is required to do the work. In describing initiation, implementation, and institutionalization, we pointed out how motivation may vary in people during these phases. Adults "need" a different set of motivators during each phase if they are to continue to grow toward expertise. When thinking about effective professional development through each phase of the life span of differentiation, two "truths" make sense to us:

• Overloading professional development at the beginning of the differentiation initiation is generally a mistake. Providing professional development over the entire life span of the change initiative is a much better fit for what adult learners need.

• The professional development provided must itself be *differentiated*. Differentiated professional development is the only way to effectively support the evolving emotions and needs of teachers who are implementing differentiation.

We advocate thinking about professional development as a constant and deliberate focus throughout the life span of the differentiation initiative. Simply put, this kind of strategic adult learning should occur formally at important junctures but also informally throughout each week of each year. The design for the adult learning will change over time in response to progress and individual teacher needs. Here is a brief illustration of the composite approach we recommend.

....

Bowertown Middle School Jumps into
Differentiation with Powerful Learning

Principal Rene Villegas carefully led his teachers into the exploration of differentiated instruction. After surveying the entire faculty, he determined that many of them were interested in gaining more fundamental knowledge of differentiation before they started implementing its strategies in the classroom. In the teacher work days before the start of the new school year, he provided training for the staff focused on broad, basic knowledge about differentiation. After school started, he provided additional team time for his teachers to discuss what they had learned during the training and any low-prep strategies they were already trying. He encouraged experimentation and individual teacher exploration of differentiation throughout the first two months of the school year.

Toward the end of the second month of work, Mr. Villegas used two successive faculty meetings to share what teachers were doing and to introduce simple grouping strategies that they might try. Again, to encourage implementation of these strategies, he offered additional faculty meeting times over the next two months, at which teachers were encouraged to share their successes and dilemmas. At these meetings, teachers also had a choice of topics they might explore, and they met in small discussion groups in the school's media center. All of these informal discussions were teacher-led. Throughout this period, Mr. Villegas, teacher specialists, and other school leaders talked with teachers about differentiation in their classrooms, team meetings, and hall conversations.

....

How many times did professional development occur during Bowertown Middle School's first semester of initiating and implementing differentiation? It's difficult to put a concrete number on it. Scattered throughout Mr. Villegas's strategic training sessions and faculty meetings were many informal opportunities, team meetings, and hallway discussions about differentiation, demonstrating the kind of seamless, job-embedded adult learning that must occur throughout initiation, implementation, and institutionalization of change. Mr. Villegas did not make the common mistake of overwhelming his teachers with training at the beginning of the initiative and then providing little support when teachers were actually beginning to implement differentiation decisions. Instead, he offered some training at the initiation of differentiation to provide broad understanding of the practices. When he sensed or observed that teachers were comfortable trying out some strategies, he created time for them to work together to share successful practices and address confounding dilemmas.

Although this kind of informal, pervasive, teacher-to-teacher professional development may be foreign to many school and district leaders, for those of us who care about the implementation of differentiation practices and making real changes in student experiences in classrooms, it is perhaps the most important kind of adult learning to promote. We will continue to develop the idea of the right "designs" for professional development for each phase of the differentiation initiative later in this chapter.

Idea #2: Effective Professional Development Is Job-Embedded and Interdependent

The most effective adult learning occurs naturally throughout the teachers' work day and is guided by the goals of results, implementation, and collaboration among professionals. This kind of "job-embedded" professional development is focused at the workplace, available to all teachers, and directly linked to actual practices. See Figure 4.1 for illustrations of the ideas behind job-embedded professional development.

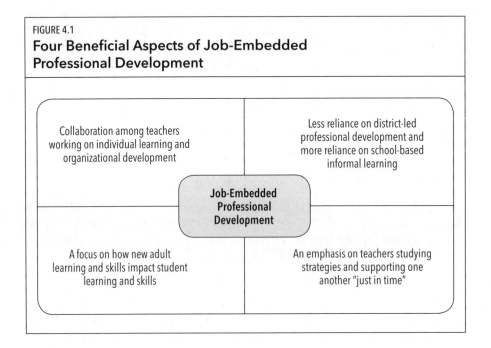

FIGURE 4.1
Four Beneficial Aspects of Job-Embedded Professional Development

Collaboration among teachers working on individual learning and organizational development

Less reliance on district-led professional development and more reliance on school-based informal learning

Job-Embedded Professional Development

A focus on how new adult learning and skills impact student learning and skills

An emphasis on teachers studying strategies and supporting one another "just in time"

Job-embedded professional development is not scattered or laissez-faire. It is deliberate and focused, but in a way that can be unfamiliar to school leaders. Rather than tell teachers what they ought to be doing, effective leaders focus on strategic actions that will support teachers as they build knowledge and develop new insight, skills, and understanding. This is what it means to grow teachers—a concept we value so much that we've incorporated it into the title of this book. "Growing teachers" involves finding opportunities for them to work together, learn with one another, and hold one another accountable for implementing what they are learning. By working collaboratively toward the ultimate vision of responsive, fully differentiated classrooms, these adult learners build a community rooted in respect and interdependence. This is an outcome that cannot be guaranteed by "training." In fact, stand-alone "training," even if it is the predominant professional development design, is the method *least* likely to achieve the vision, because it is the furthest removed from the actual workplace.

Central to the idea of powerful, collaborative, job-embedded professional study and development is the idea of "interdependence" (Little, 2008). If professional development is to effectively support ongoing differentiation efforts, it must be must be deliberately designed to promote the faculty's mutual reliance on one another. With clear guidance regarding targets, structures for collaboration, and hands-on support from one another, the entire faculty will advance both their understanding of differentiation and their capacity to problem solve when differentiating in their classrooms. Interdependence is not easy, however. As Little (2008) reminds us, "The ability of a group to both influence individual practice and collective practice is contingent on aims held in common. Without some kind of foundational commitment to ambitious kinds of practice, the likelihood of the group having influence on that kind of practice is probably small" (p. 54).

This caution takes us back to two critical concepts: (1) how important it is to keep people motivated to work toward differentiation and (2) how powerful the vision, operational vision, and change plans are in identifying the ambitious kinds of practice that will coalesce teams around meaningful learning and collaborative practice.

The dilemmas facing those who design professional development are numerous and daunting. Our third guiding idea, then, focuses on fundamentals for creating professional development that will help promote deep learning.

Idea #3: Effective Professional Development Reflects Standards for Motivated Adult Learning

Learning Forward, an international organization dedicated to quality professional development, suggests that the designers of professional development base their plans on seven standards for effective adult learning (Learning Forward, 2011). Figure 4.2 presents our interpretation of how each of these standards relates to the initiation, implementation, and institutionalization of differentiation in schools.

FIGURE 4.2

Learning Forward's Adult Learning Standards Applied to Professional Development for Differentiation

Adult Learning Standard	Core Elements	Our Interpretation
1. The most effective professional development occurs within **learning communities** that are committed to continuous improvement, collective responsibility, and goal alignment.	When moving to implementation, job-embedded professional learning must be a component, emphasizing individual adult learning, group learning, and cohesive action.	As teachers move toward differentiated practices, they will need to rely on not only individual planning but also team accountability for action and results.
2. **Leadership** must constantly build systems to support continuous adult learning and experimentation.	Leaders must carefully plan professional development to support implementation, and must model their support for high-quality adult learning.	Long-term differentiation takes time, and the implementation will fall apart if leaders do not create a strategic system for supporting not only adult learning but also implementation of their ideas.
3. The prioritization, monitoring, and coordination of **resources** are critical to professional development.	Time, technology, schedules, and materials are all critical elements of ongoing adult learning.	Much professional development for differentiation occurs at the beginning of the initiative; for differentiation to be effective over time, the resources must be more carefully distributed and evaluated.
4. Information and ongoing **data** are critical for leaders if they are to plan, assess, and evaluate effective adult learning plans.	Ongoing use of data and information will be critical to leaders to determine what kind of professional development is needed and why.	For leaders to know how professional development can assist teachers in implementing differentiation, they will need to constantly assess the progress the school is making toward the differentiation vision.
5. Different **learning designs** that integrate the best of what we know about research, adult change, and efficient models are necessary for effective professional development.	There are a variety of professional development models and designs that work effectively, depending on the needs of the participants.	Professional development for differentiation may focus first on the elements of differentiation; however, later the model must shift to one supporting trial, experimentation, collective planning, and collaboration.
6. There must be sustained support for **implementation** of the practices that are learned.	School leaders must understand how change occurs over time and how implementation is driven by motivational principles.	Although the vision for differentiation describes it in its most refined state, the leader must use "change plans" to describe each stage of implementation for practitioners.
7. Effective professional development must be aligned with the **outcomes** of educator performance and curriculum standards.	Leaders must make the case for how the professional development is connected and linked to the mandates for educator performance and powerful student curriculum.	Leaders must see clear connections among professional development, the purpose of differentiation, and how differentiation is aligned with educator evaluation and student performance. These connections must also be clear to teachers.

For a look at how these standards can guide the way a school leader thinks about, plans, and manages the professional development necessary to launch and maintain schoolwide differentiation, we'll revisit Mr. Villegas at Bowertown Middle School.

Mr. Villegas Incorporates Adult Learning Standards into His Plans for Professional Development

When Bowertown began the implementation phase of its differentiation initiative, Mr. Villegas knew his staff needed to know more about the fundamentals of differentiated instruction. He made a conscious decision to focus on training as the most efficient model for disseminating that information (Learning Designs). However, he also knew that after this initial training, he would need to shift his focus away from formal professional development into a more job-embedded model where teachers could meet, share their ideas on differentiation, and support one another as they began to incorporate more differentiated practices (Learning Communities).

To that end, he scheduled regular meetings, giving teachers released time from their classrooms so that they could meet, share, and discuss (Learning Designs, Leadership). As these informal meetings progressed through the first two months of the school year, Mr. Villegas worked to stay on top of his teachers' material needs through informal conversations and facultywide surveys. To that end, he strategically purchased books, videos, and other resources to support teachers' efforts to create and implement differentiated lesson plans (Resources).

Mr. Villegas encouraged teachers to share actual results from their differentiated teaching practices at these informal, teacher-led meetings. As the semester wore on and teachers had more and more results to share, he provided a quick, informal protocol for them to use as they examine and interpret examples of student work (Implementation, Data).

Midway through the semester, at one of the faculty meetings, Mr. Villegas asked teachers to share their reflections on the work they had been doing. Using "tickets out the door" and follow-up focus groups, he and his leadership team gathered informal but powerful data about the beginning implementation of the differentiation initiative. They used these data in their mid-semester leadership meeting to chart additional support, resources, and learning designs to support continued focus and implementation of differentiated practices in the classrooms (Outcomes).

This scenario illustrates how one school leader's thinking and actions were driven by his knowledge of the seven guiding standards for professional learning. We suggest that professional development for differentiation would be so much more effective and efficient if these standards became part of the active repertoire of each of us as we lead the change.

Teachers facing the demands of differentiation may be more likely to sustain their efforts when school leaders design ongoing professional development that capitalizes on not only the Learning Forward standards but also the elements of human motivation we discussed in Chapter 2—autonomy, purpose, and mastery. In tackling the challenges of differentiation, astute leaders incorporate long-term plans that build choice (*autonomy*), relevance (*purpose*), and practice (*mastery*) into their professional development designs. Our feeling is that when leaders undergird their professional development plans with the tenets of motivation, teachers are encouraged, through more effective professional development, to develop the "growth" portion of their thinking. Dedicated to growth and firmly supported through powerful professional development, the teachers can commit to the promises of differentiation and demonstrate through their study, effort, and collaboration that they can achieve more and more in the classroom so students will benefit.

Idea #4: Adults Can Develop Mastery of New Practices over Time, Through Strategic Support

There is, then, a direct application of the concept of "growth accomplishment" to professional development. The ideas of growing individual learning and accomplishment, and attending to each individual's growth pathway begin to align with the zone of proximal development first introduced by Lev Vygotsky (1980, 1986). Vygotsky described this zone as the distance that exists between the actual level of knowledge and skill and the potential level of development a learner might achieve if supported by either adult guidance or interactions with equal or more capable peers. Although Vygotsky's work applied to children and traditional classroom educational settings and is fundamental for differentiating for student readiness, his ideas are also very useful when thinking about professional development. The concept of the zone of proximal development illustrates that the way that any of us learn to do things is in small steps, starting from where we are right now. Complicated skills aren't mastered in a single afternoon, which is why adult learners don't suddenly acquire a body of knowledge and the skills necessary to implement differentiated instruction after a single afternoon training session (Shapiro, 2011).

Vygotsky's work describes the relationship that exists between the current "state" of an individual's knowledge and skill and the kind of support that can result in the deeper development of those skills and in greater accomplishment. In essence, professional development exists to help people move from their current state to deeper knowledge and skills and to the independent and sophisticated application of that knowledge and those skills. The idea of moving from the current state and simple "learning" to the independent, sophisticated application of the practice has, in the instructional realm, become known as the gradual release of responsibility (Pearson & Gallagher, 1983).

The concepts behind the gradual release of responsibility were originally framed by Vygotsky and then developed by Pearson and Gallagher (1983). It is an optimal learning model through which responsibility for mastery shifts gradually over time. In the case of classroom instruction, the shift over time is from the teacher to the student, who will, in a step-wise fashion, ultimately be able to demonstrate independent mastery and use of the knowledge, skills, and understanding first communicated and demonstrated by the teacher. Figure 4.3 (adapted from Murphy, 2010) provides an overview of the gradual release of responsibility framework as it applies to adult learners.

Although we know this model was developed to demonstrate how students acquire mastery, it also relates to how we help *adults* develop mastery over time. Let's think specifically about its implications for conceptualizing professional development that will help an entire faculty move toward differentiation by looking at each stage of the model and identifying the pitfalls that often accompany the design of poorly planned professional learning.

The Gradual Release of Responsibility Framework

Modeled support ("I do"). The first stage is characterized by the highest degree of support and the least amount of control for the staff member. This is the phase of learning in which the school leader initiates, models, explains, thinks aloud, and begins to develop an understanding of the major components of the initiative. Often, the "modeled support" of an initiative is little more than an information session announcing the initiative. Teachers are expected to listen, learn about the initiative, and

FIGURE 4.3
**The Gradual Release of Responsibility Model
Applied to Adult Learners**

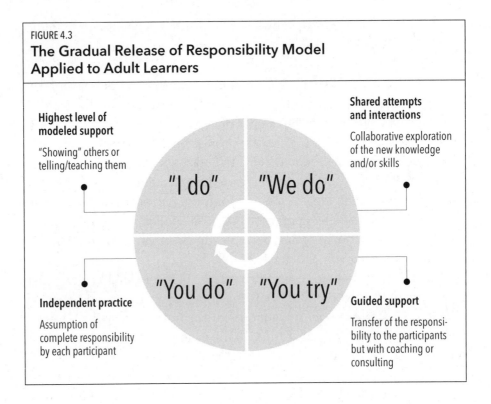

Highest level of modeled support

"Showing" others or telling/teaching them

Shared attempts and interactions

Collaborative exploration of the new knowledge and/or skills

"I do"   "We do"

"You do"   "You try"

Independent practice

Assumption of complete responsibility by each participant

Guided support

Transfer of the responsibility to the participants but with coaching or consulting

perhaps participate in the conversation or implement a portion of the learning on a very limited basis. The school leader or trainer assumes the majority of the responsibility for the initiative and asks the teachers to assume very little responsibility other than gaining general knowledge of and developing positive attitudes about the work to come.

Shared attempts and interactions ("We do"). The second stage of the model features moderate support for the teachers, who are asked to exercise some control over their learning. However, the school leader (perhaps the principal but perhaps also a long-term professional developer or an instructional specialist, such as a reading, special education, English language, or gifted education teacher) is still demonstrating, suggesting, explaining, and responding. Teachers are listening but also interacting and experimenting with ideas on a limited basis.

Guided support ("You try"). This is the stage during which the leader, professional developer, or specialist hands over more of the responsibility. There is a low level of support for the teachers, each of whom is now exercising moderate control over implementation of the initiative components. In effect, this stage is like independent practice for the teacher while the leader is watching, encouraging, clarifying, evaluating, and stepping in to re-teach as needed.

Independent practice ("You do"). In the final, fourth stage of the model, each teacher assumes independent responsibility for using the initiative components. The school leader is still giving support but is not directly involved in teaching. Rather, he or she is watching, encouraging, acknowledging, and determining additional resources to support each teacher's ability to continue implementing the initiative with a great degree of autonomy.

We are wise to pay attention to the implications of the zone of proximal development and the gradual release of responsibility model. As we design effective and appropriate professional development for differentiation, growing teachers from the first stage ("I do" or "Let me show you") to the final one ("You do") requires thoughtful analysis of the factors discussed in this chapter. If we expect too much independence too early, we can undermine the learning process, withholding support for experimentation and mastery that teachers need, and expecting effective independent implementation before it is appropriate to do so. It is extraordinarily common to see early professional development on differentiation accompanied by the expectation that teachers will move immediately to implement differentiation in their classrooms. Leaders who design professional development in that way doom differentiation to superficial attempts, short-term frustration, and ultimate failure.

Dig Deep: Think about a major initiative at your school that was supported by professional development. Did the components of this professional development lead the participants through all four stages of the gradual release of responsibility model, or did it seem to jump too quickly from the "I do" stage to the "You do" stage? What was the result of the professional development? Try using the gradual release of responsibility model to either explain its success or describe its failure.

Effective adult professional learning for differentiation capitalizes on the zone of proximal development by starting with what the adults *can* do. Then, through careful professional development designs and a system of standards-based supports and leadership, adults look for areas in which they can learn new knowledge and implement improved differentiated practices with the assistance of colleagues. In this way, change is supported and sustained. Understanding how people learn requires leaders to generate differentiated professional development designs that can help move people through the "I do" to "You do" stages so that each teacher can consistently take his or her own next steps in growth. Similar to how it is with students in a classroom, rarely will all members of a faculty be ready for each of the four states at the same time.

What Are Effective Professional Development Designs to Support the Move to Differentiation?

As the school leader considers (1) where the school is in its journey toward differentiation, (2) the principles underlying powerful professional development, (3) the seven standards guiding how to lead professional development, and (4) the "distance" between teachers' current points of development and the vision for their practice, a practical question emerges: "What professional development designs will be most effective in supporting teacher growth?"

The answer is not algorithmic. Many factors influence the design of professional development. They include, but are not limited to, the goals of adult learning, the amount of trust and collaboration among the adult learners, their familiarity with the principles and practices of the various elements of differentiation, the urgency and the magnitude of the change, and available resources (Murphy, 2014).

In addition, leaders must consider the strengths and limitations of the professional development designs themselves. Each design carries with it a bias about how people will learn and develop their skills, beliefs, and attitudes. Each design is connected to objectives that are indigenous to the design itself. Each design implies how it might be assessed and measured in terms of its effectiveness with the participating adults. Lastly, each design is somehow connected with learning, implementation, and student results. Consider a few effective professional development designs in Figure 4.4 and reflect on each design's elements and underlying premises.

These professional development designs become our tool kit as we reflect on our intent for the learning. Examples of these designs in action help us see the power in professional development. For instance, the goal of the training design is to build knowledge, understanding, and skill. The attributes of training also support the likelihood of group clarity on the knowledge or skill, because training can be delivered to a large number of people at one time. In the gradual release of responsibility

FIGURE 4.4

A Collection of Effective Professional Development Designs

Professional Development Design	Description of the Design	Factors to Consider Before Choosing
Training, Courses, Seminars	Highly structured professional development far removed from the classroom context, selected when it is determined that a large number of staff members need to learn from an "expert" to quickly gain knowledge or awareness.	• The urgency of the change and necessity of quick acquisition of knowledge or awareness • The need for application of practice (training is not necessarily linked to actual application of practice) • The plan to support the application of practice after the training
Immersion	An inquiry-based design in which teachers are "immersed" in the activities they would be asking students to engage in. Typically, immersion is accomplished at schools where teachers "work through" materials, kits, and textbooks together, creating and experiencing the same kinds of assignments and activities they will ask students to perform. Immersion is useful for gaining knowledge, awareness, and providing reflection time.	• Time for teacher collaboration and practice • The commitment teachers have to application • Trust among the teachers • Support for resources to focus the immersion
Curriculum Development and Implementation	Teachers working together to either develop new lesson plans or strengthen/revise previous practice. Curriculum development is useful for developing new knowledge about a content area and providing practice for implementation of the new plans within a collegial setting.	• Time for curriculum development, discussion, and implementation • Ongoing support for application • Trust and history of communication and dialogue among the practicing teachers • The extent of "problem solving" that teachers must accomplish and the practicality of their demands
Analyzing Student Work	Examining samples of student work and products in order to understand students' thinking and learning strategies around an idea or concept. The study of the work leads to further decisions about appropriate teaching strategies, re-teaching, and materials selection. Design is particularly effective in supporting reflection, new knowledge, and awareness.	• Commitment to a unified assignment and the selection of work samples to review • Trust and history of communication and commitment to experimenting with new strategies • Time for review and conversation • Whether or not the initiative is in full implementation

(Cont.)

FIGURE 4.4

A Collection of Effective Professional Development Designs –(*continued*)

Professional Development Design	Description of the Design	Factors to Consider Before Choosing
Case Analyses	Case analyses can include case studies, video clips, and so on. The examination presents a "real-life" scenario in which teacher practice is discussed, deliberated, with implications in terms of issues or outcomes. Case analyses are effective for reflection and the acquisition of knowledge.	• Materials and resources for cases • Time for extended review and conversations • Trust and history of communication skills among the participating teachers
Mentoring and Coaching	Usually one-on-one with equally or more experienced teacher to improve teaching and learning via feedback, observation and conversation, problem solving, or co-planning. Mentoring and coaching are particularly effective when the goal includes practice, knowledge, or reflection.	• Human resources • The levels of trust throughout the organization • A history of conversation and problem solving • Peer-to-peer collaboration and comfort
Study Groups and Book Studies	Related study groups and book studies involve small groups in regular, structured, and collaborative interactions regarding topics identified by the group or by the book/resource being used. Book studies are particularly useful for awareness and knowledge. Study groups have a bias toward implementation of the new practice after the learning; they are useful if the goal for professional development includes knowledge, awareness, practice, and/or reflection.	• Fiscal resources for the materials to be examined and studied • Time for study and collaboration • Trust among staff members • History of peer-to-peer work
Action Research	Disciplined action research involves locating a problem area in student learning, collecting data about the problem, studying relevant resources, deciding to take action, and then studying the results in terms of future action or decision making. Action research is particularly useful for knowledge, practice, and reflection.	• History of peer-to-peer work • Trust regarding sharing of practice • Time for study and collaboration • Relevant when the initiative is in full implementation

framework, training sits squarely in the "I do" stage, for it requires the most from the trainer and the least from the participant. Training is often incorporated into professional development at the beginning stages of differentiation, as the goal is usually to bring people closer to a common language and understanding of some of differentiation's undergirding principles and practices. Therefore, under certain conditions, training can be an excellent design for disseminating carefully constructed knowledge and skills to participants.

Compare the attributes and uses of training with study groups, which can be another effective design under certain conditions. Study groups are small, focused groups of professionals who come together to study a topic, implement changes based on their study, and assess the results. Study groups require a sense of "team," relying on the strongest elements of collegial collaboration to make the design successful. Again, in the gradual release of responsibility framework, study groups live somewhere in between the "We do" and the "You try" stages. Because of the collaborative spirit of the design, study groups must have at their core a shared focus, common relevance, and trust among the participants, since the nature of the groups asks individuals to share their teaching practices and results. Study groups can be incorporated in the initial stages of differentiation professional development, but they may well be *more* suitable when teachers are in the beginning stages of implementation of their strategies. Study groups, when incorporated during implementation and when functioning effectively, become a regularly scheduled structure to support teachers as they troubleshoot differentiation ideas and bring results back to the group for analysis and additional commitments to move further into differentiation (again, "We do" and "You try").

The fluidity and complexity of thinking and planning required for professional development suggests that there is no perfect professional development design. Instead, the designs must work coherently to support teacher development throughout the life span of learning about and implementing differentiation. Because of this need to think in coherent ways about professional development for the long term, wise school leaders incorporate multiple designs in their overall professional development planning and implementation, as evidenced by the example of Mr. Villegas at Bowertown Middle School. Professional development, then, becomes one type of glue that holds together the principles and practices of differentiation through the years of full implementation, changing along the way to link teachers' needs and the goals of differentiation.

Reflect and Assess: So far, our exploration of professional development has covered a lot of ground, including thinking about professional development as something to be provided throughout the "life span" of differentiation, the nature of effective professional development, using standards based on the adult zone of proximal development and how that relates to professional development, and professional development designs that work under certain conditions. How do all of these ideas influence your thinking about professional development? How do these ideas influence how you will plan professional development for differentiation? What designs are you thinking about using in your plans for differentiation? If you had to summarize how your leadership will be altered to support professional development for differentiation, what would you say to teachers? What would you say to your supervisors? What would you say to your community leaders and families?

What Concerns Will Teachers Have as They Learn About and Begin to Implement Differentiation?

The purpose of professional development is not adult knowledge or skill acquisition for its own sake; it's the application that matters. What really concerns us is the doing—the implementation of powerful differentiation practices and the student learning that results. For this reason, it makes sense to refocus on the role that teachers play in creating differentiated schools, and reflect on the concerns they are likely to have about this change initiative, which range from wariness about the intellectual and pragmatic challenges of designing and delivering new lesson plans to the emotional challenge of exploring their own personal zone of proximal development. If these concerns aren't addressed, they may have a debilitating effect on professional development. To put it bluntly, adult emotional reactions to change, even those that seem unreasonable to us, can derail the most carefully planned initiatives.

Adult concerns about school change have been written about extensively. Hall and Hord (2001) refer to "Stages of Concern," which "give us a way of thinking about people's feelings and perceptions about change" (p. 57). The authors describe these changes in four broad categories:

• **Unrelated concerns** seem to be more powerful than concerns about implementation of differentiation. They may focus more on the teachers' particular circumstances, and they seem more prevalent and important than any concerns related to learning about or implementing differentiation in the school. We find that, although unrelated concerns may not be directly related to implementing differentiation, they can sometimes distract teachers from the work at hand and create resistance to change.

• **Self concerns** most often appear when people are *first* learning about or implementing differentiation. Self concerns are all about "me" and whether or not "I" can succeed. These concerns also tend to magnify teachers' responses to the fairness of what is being demanded of them as individuals. Our experience is that self concerns are often triggered by demands on personal time and energy, and these demands are often exaggerated by perceptions of comparative pressure on others. In other words, teachers may exhibit self concerns because they believe the demands on them are much more intense than on others.

• **Task concerns** appear when the actual work and press for implementation become clear to all. Task concerns are usually about the work of differentiation. At this point, teachers are focusing on getting the job done well. When people are feeling strong task concerns, they want more strategies in time management, student management, set up, schedule management, and so on. We believe that strong task concerns in a school are a combination of good news and bad news. The good news is that people are implementing differentiation; the bad news is that they are having a bit of trouble with managing it all.

• **Impact concerns** focus more on what's happening with students and how teaching can be altered to better reach more students. Here, concerns have shifted away from "us" and from the task, focusing instead on student performance resulting from their differentiated practices.

Not surprisingly, through the progression of a change initiative from initiation to full implementation, multiple kinds of concerns may appear at once. Usually, however, there will be a predominant category that a majority of teachers are exhibiting at a given time (Hall & Hord, 2001).

A detailed set of Hall and Hord's seven Stages of Concern is provided in Figure 4.5. Note that the descriptions include the category of concern as well as how expressions of each stage might sound to the leader responsible for implementing differentiation.

Assessing teacher concerns about differentiation is vital to the planning and management of powerful professional development. Attention to these concerns propels us into informal conversations with teachers

FIGURE 4.5

The Stages of Concern Applied to Long-Term Change

Category	Stage	Stage Name	Description	What It Sounds Like
Impact	6	**Refocusing**	Teachers understand the broader benefits of the innovation and are interested in considering broad alterations or adaptations to make the initiative work even better.	"Differentiation is working well. I think I have some ideas that would make it even better for our kids."
	5	**Collaboration**	Teachers are interested and desire to work with others on the changes–sharing ideas and cooperating with others to make impact on students even greater.	"Can our team work with the other teams on this? We have some ideas about how we are implementing the changes but want to hear from others about their perspectives."
	4	**Consequence**	The teachers at this stage have shifted their concerns from management to students–they are now looking at how the initiative is affecting students, which students are affected by the changes, and what kinds of adaptations might be necessary.	"I can see the results now with my kids. I believe they are understanding mathematics better. I'm looking to see how I can tweak the initiative to benefit their learning even more."
Task	3	**Management**	At this stage, teachers are more influenced by their concerns related to "doing" the initiative–including the processes and tasks of actually implementing the change in its first steps. The concerns are about time, efficiency, management, and scheduling.	"I can't seem to get all of it done in the time I have for math. It's taking so long to write my lesson plans and form groups!"
Self	2	**Personal**	The concerns teachers have focus on the personal demands of the change and whether or not the individual feels adequate to take on the change. Concerns are about perceived rewards, conflicts, and decision making about the change.	"I look at all that is required of me and I have to wonder: Where do I start? Differentiation seems complicated! Can I do this? Is it worth it? Who decided we have to do this?"
	1	**Informational**	Teachers want more information about the change. The concern is that they do not know enough detail about the components of the initiative, and they want to learn more about it and what will be demanded of them.	"I'm not sure I understand it. I'd like to learn more before I can commit to doing it. What is differentiation, exactly?"
Awareness	0	**Awareness**	There is little involvement with the initiative or little desire to learn more about it.	"This too will pass. This is another one of the district's big ideas that will fail."

and small groups to determine the kinds of concerns they have. Armed with this valuable information, we can determine the current change context in which teachers are living and the potential dangers and barriers they face as they attempt to maintain their focus on and energy for differentiation. Most importantly, we can take steps to provide professional development activities that address the specific issues our teachers are facing, reducing the intensity of their concerns and encouraging them to move past task issues and begin to notice the impact of their efforts on student outcomes.

We will revisit the Stages of Concern in Chapter 6, when we offer suggestions for assessing teachers' reactions to differentiation efforts that are under way and using these reactions to evaluate progress. For now, however, consider this example of a leader who leveraged her understanding of teacher concerns to modify her professional development plans.

Dr. Bennett Uses the Stages of Concern to Create More Effective Professional Development

Early in the development of differentiated instruction practices at her high school, Principal Eve Bennett mapped out a training plan for her entire staff. Her aim was to equip all of her teachers with foundational understandings of differentiated instruction. The first step of this training was conducted over a three-day summer seminar. The teachers explored some of the major tenets of differentiation and watched video clips of these concepts in action. They were challenged to continue their individual study of differentiation through study groups, which would continue throughout the fall semester. At the end of the summer session, Dr. Bennett asked teachers to respond to these questions as their "ticket out the door": *When I think about what I have learned about differentiation and how we are going to begin to implement differentiated practices throughout the fall, what am I still worried about? What are my most pressing concerns?*

Teachers were encouraged to write as much as they wanted on their index cards and submit them without signing them. After Dr. Bennett had collected these cards, interpreted each person's most pressing concerns, and categorized them, she concluded that the great majority of concerns (about two-thirds) were informational, about 20 percent of the other concerns were personal, and a few teachers were already concerned about the tasks and how to manage them. In other words, most of the concerns were "self" in nature.

This information gave Dr. Bennett great insight into her teachers' affective response to the initiative. Knowing that the majority of them had concerns in terms of either wanting more information about requirements or wondering "if they could do differentiation," Dr. Bennett focused early faculty meetings that fall on questions and answers, examples, clarifying the operational vision for differentiation, and supporting small steps toward implementation in order to build individual confidence.

Dr. Bennett's knowledge and use of the Stages of Concern did not end with this one-shot analysis. In successive weeks, she incorporated the stages in ongoing, informal talks with individual teachers through "one-legged interviews," detailed in Chapter 6 (see p. 116). In these short but focused conversations, Dr. Bennett found that the concerns teachers were facing, predictably, had changed. By mid-fall, the majority of the most pressing concerns were in terms of "doing the work of differentiation," or task concerns. She was delighted that she had scheduled study groups to support teachers, and she began to strengthen the focus of those study groups toward tasks, leadership in differentiated classrooms, establishing and managing flexible classroom routines, assigning students to flexible groups, analyzing formative assessments, and so on.

Dr. Bennett's thinking provides a good example of the reality that professional development for differentiation must itself be differentiated. Our quick analysis of her guidance yields multiple factors she considered as she led professional development at her school. These professional development practices were evident as she launched and supported change toward effective differentiation. In this scenario, Dr. Bennett

• Understood and used what she knew about the "life span" of differentiation implementation. She knew that during initiation, teachers would have predictable concerns. She also used her knowledge of the global Learning Forward standards to guide not only her planning for differentiation but also the design and support of the professional development needed to launch the change.

• Knew that her teachers needed to understand the purpose for the changes. She also was comfortable encouraging teachers to make decisions about practices they might begin to use.

• Realized that teachers' concerns would shift as they began using differentiation. To support this, she created study groups that were informal, job-embedded, and focused on the "doing" of the work.

• Incorporated varieties of professional development designs as she moved from late summer to the fall implementation of differentiation.

• Used the Stages of Concern to frequently assess teacher concerns, shared this evidence with her leadership team, and adjusted her plans.

As we suggested at the beginning of this chapter, there is no recipe for powerful professional development to support an initiative such as differentiation. Deep, important, successful differentiated practices require time, energy, focus, and a grasp of the concepts illustrated in this chapter. As with all great implementation stories, various factors and individual school and district contexts heavily influence the nature of the professional development that results in teacher changes and student results.

Cultivating Leadership Competencies

Think about your status with the following concepts as you develop your efforts to implement differentiation. In particular, reflect on the professional development practices you see as the key drivers in movement toward effective differentiation schoolwide. As you do this, consider the elements listed below. What must you learn in order to create and sustain powerful adult learning opportunities for your teachers? How can you design the learning opportunities that will build on what we know about change and focus teachers on the core principles and practices of differentiation?

❏ There is a clear set of beliefs that drives our professional learning design and efforts toward schoolwide differentiation.

❏ The professional development that is delivered focuses on results, is job-embedded, and embodies high standards for quality adult learning.

❏ There is more emphasis on implementing effective differentiation than just learning about it.

❏ The professional development design is carefully planned to support beginning learning, implementation, and refinement of differentiation practices.

❏ Teachers' concerns about new differentiation practices are regularly assessed and interpreted.

 Download

5

Engaging in Productive Conversations That Nourish Growth

To this point, we have looked at a variety of critical components in leading successful initiatives to implement schoolwide differentiation. They include the following:

- The power of both developing relationships and focusing on results.
- How differentiation may evolve as it becomes fully institutionalized.
- What motivates people to continue the work in differentiated instruction until it is deeply implemented.
- How to create an operational vision for differentiation and yearly change plans to manage the work toward that vision.
- The kind of professional development that supports differentiation.
- Different professional development designs that work to support differentiation.
- How teachers' concerns can be both understood and addressed over time.

When employing these components in leadership work, it's important to keep everyone moving forward while also ensuring that everyone has a sense of "where they are" in their own work. The simplest and perhaps the most valuable tool we as school leaders have for gauging progress and motivating individuals toward their next steps is regular, ongoing conversation with each teacher and staff member. When these conversations are planned and conducted in a manner that builds relationships while maintaining a focus on practice and results, we are exercising three critical practices in school improvement through our "talk" about differentiation:

- **Leading** differentiation through talking about the purpose of differentiation and how the individual is moving closer and closer to the **vision** for differentiation.
- **Learning** about the current state of differentiated instruction through questions designed to build the individual's **understanding** of the current state of differentiation.
- **Assessing** progress by delving into both the emotional **responses** to this comprehensive change and the quality of changes in classroom practice.

Too often, leaders haven't had the chance to learn how to plan and conduct their conversations in this strategic way—to lead, learn, and assess. Conversations about initiatives such as differentiation should be front and center in our minds, yet too frequently we relegate purposeful conversations about the work as something we'll do when we can find the time. Or, instead of understanding and employing the power of conversation, we look at it as something to check off for required summative evaluation. It's no wonder that, to teachers, the way current evaluation systems link talk about teaching and a performance rating can feel like an intellectual and emotional ambush. In the end, the feeling devalues their perception of conversations that could be meaningful and motivating.

What's needed is something quite different: leaders and teachers should engage in regular formal and informal conversations about differentiation. These conversations must occur frequently enough that all parties come to see them as a natural part of practice and something that's simply necessary in order to lead, learn, and assess how differentiation efforts are improving student outcomes. This chapter discusses how to plan and lead frequent conversations in a variety of settings in order to strengthen leader–teacher relationships and enhance our ability to lead, learn, and assess.

What Are Typical Leader–Teacher Conversations Like?

Leader–teacher conversations generally fall into a predictable pattern, unfolding in terms of who holds the power and information. Teachers tend to perceive themselves as unequal conversation participants, because it's the leader who sets the agenda and has the information, and the teachers suspect this information will be used, however politely, to maneuver them into changing what they do in the classroom. The teacher's job is to sit at the conference table, receive the leader's "suggestions," and commit to some kind of action that will satisfy the leader. The motivation for change is entirely external, solely depending on power, position, or reward. Although this type of conversation may lead to short-term changes, it does little to engage the teacher in deep thinking or participative decision making.

This characterization of common conversations between leader and teacher is definitely negative, yet we find it typical of what tends to happen during leader–teacher talk. Such conversations do very little to support the development of the relationship so critical to sustained improvement in differentiated instruction. In many cases, instead of the teacher eagerly seeking the leader's information and diving deeply into the meaning of it, the teacher spends the time nodding or saying what's expected while silently carrying on an entirely different explanatory or defensive conversation in his or her own head. In all cases, when a conversation is unbalanced in terms of information, control, or power, the outcome will be less focused and more temporary, and it may be debilitating to the less powerful party.

Findings from a recent Tennessee Department of Education study seem to support the notion that unproductive conversations are the unfortunate norm. When 2,100 teachers representing a range of tenure statuses, accomplishments, and previous summative evaluation scores were asked about the impact leader-led feedback conversations had on their classroom practices, 16–22 percent (it varied based on years of experience and overall evaluative ranking) reported that they didn't change *any* of their classroom practices or behaviors as a result of the feedback conversations with their leader. When probed for reasons for their inaction, the teachers reported that (1) during the conversations they did not develop any definite ideas on what to improve, (2) the feedback was so vague that they could not get a sense of what they could do differently, or (3) they did not think the changes suggested would really help students (Tennessee Department of Education, 2013).

It doesn't have to be this way. When conversations about instructional practice are less summative and more formative—and when they're frequent, specific, and well-informed and function in a way that builds the relationship between the leader and teacher—they're more likely to be seen as helpful and more likely to actually help. These conversations send teachers the message that their leader is listening. What the leader is doing is differentiating his or her conversation to match each teacher's needs.

What Characterizes Productive Conversations About Differentiation?

With the power of conversation established, the next logical question is, "What do productive conversations about differentiation look like? How can leaders plan them so they are efficient and effective?"

Danielson (2009) provides some good insight to start us off. "What is important is that the conversation is enhanced by the skill of those conducting it to dig below the surface, to help teachers examine underlying assumptions and likely consequences of different approaches," she writes. "With skilled facilitation, conversations can help a teacher reflect deeply on [his or her] practice and see patterns of both student behavior and the results of teacher actions" (p. 1). In these two sentences, Danielson has turned up the volume on great teaching conversations, pointing out that they are structured to go deep into the work, require both parties to examine their theories of what works with students, and involve brainstorming a variety of approaches that might get better results. We would add one more element to this description: great teaching conversations also lead to decisions about what the next *actions* should be and the commitment of both parties to take those actions in classrooms.

In this way, the "best" conversations are cyclical, characterized by recurring elements of thinking, interpreting, brainstorming, acting, and then starting over again by thinking about and interpreting the results of the new actions. Our notion of a great conversation is influenced by the idea of the continual, intertwined focus on both building a relationship with the teacher and on action and results. In planning a powerful conversation, we have two simultaneous foci: *what* we want the conversation to accomplish, and *how* we want the conversation to feel and be perceived. Figure 5.1 illustrates this layered approach. The top portion of the figure represents the "what," and the bottom represents the "how."

Let's look first at the "what." Each productive conversation about differentiation will involve the following four actions:

1. Information discovery. The conversation must invite the teacher into an exploration of shared information or current approaches he or she is taking to address students' varied learning needs.

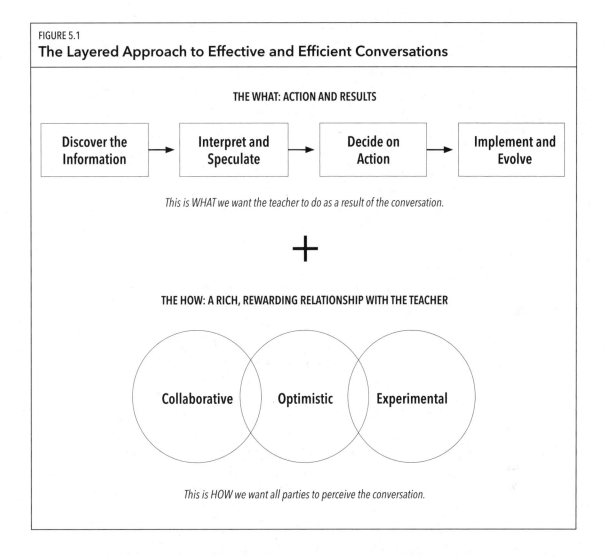

FIGURE 5.1
The Layered Approach to Effective and Efficient Conversations

THE WHAT: ACTION AND RESULTS

| Discover the Information | → | Interpret and Speculate | → | Decide on Action | → | Implement and Evolve |

This is WHAT we want the teacher to do as a result of the conversation.

+

THE HOW: A RICH, REWARDING RELATIONSHIP WITH THE TEACHER

Collaborative   Optimistic   Experimental

This is HOW we want all parties to perceive the conversation.

2. Interpretation and speculation. While reviewing the shared information, we must invite the teacher to articulate his or her current approaches and current results, as well as talk about new strategies that might be most advantageous to try next.

3. Decision and action. The conversation must lead to some kind of decision and selection of something to try out in order to deepen the practice of differentiated instruction in the teacher's classroom.

4. Implementation and evolution. The conversation must involve a commitment by both parties to do what each needs to do to get the action under way. It must also reinforce the idea that working with the new approach is intended to evolve the teacher's practice and lay the groundwork for permanent classroom change.

The "how" of productive leader–teacher conversations concerns how we want them to feel. In intent and perception, we want them to be

• **Collaborative.** There must be a genuine attention to a collaborative, side-by-side spirit and an appreciation of one another's opinions.

• **Optimistic.** Both people in the conversation must feel that the talk is about what *can* be done, not a rehashing of problems or reasons *not* to move ahead. In addition, the leader must convey a sense of optimism about the teacher's capacity to bring about a change and receive the necessary support.

• **Experimental.** All great conversations have a *try-it-out* feel. The talk should focus on possible actions and a way to enact actions in terms of real, concrete, attainable steps.

Let's take a look at these elements in play.

James Brooks and Melinda Peretti Engage in Productive Conversation

Northside Elementary School is in the second full year of a differentiation initiative and, in the judgment of Principal James Brooks, the implementation stage is progressing positively. Today, Mr. Brooks seeks a quick, informal conversation with Melinda Peretti, a 3rd grade teacher with three years of experience. Ms. Peretti is developing her skills in differentiated instruction and has demonstrated a willingness to try alternate strategies and assess her students' resulting progress.

Conversations about differentiation happen all the time at Northside, so Mr. Brooks simply sends an e-mail to Ms. Peretti asking for permission to drop by her classroom during her planning time to touch base with her on the work. She has time today and is waiting for Mr. Brooks when he arrives.

In Ms. Peretti's classroom, Mr. Brooks opens with casual chat, asking Ms. Peretti about her family and work in general and listening mindfully. Soon, though, the talk turns to the matter at hand. "When you think about differentiated instruction in your classroom, how would you describe the progress you are making?" he asks.

Ms. Peretti begins to tick off the practices that she's been using regularly, explaining that she feels able to implement them smoothly. Probing a bit, the principal asks her to focus on the students and describe the impact these practices are having on them. She begins her reflection by naming the practices that she has seen improve her students' engagement and ability to access content and eventually comes around to practices that have not had the effect she'd hoped for—areas that she wants to improve (interest centers, differentiated homework, and peer tutoring)

Mr. Brooks encourages her to continue thinking about these areas. Together they begin to brainstorm additional practices and alternate ways to try out these practices. After a few minutes, Mr. Brooks guides Ms. Peretti to focus on her next steps. He asks her to choose one or two of the ideas they have discussed and develop a short-term plan for trying the strategies. As the conversation ends, he alludes to how each of her short-term goals helps Ms. Peretti get closer to the school's yearly change plan for differentiation and also notes ways he can continue to support her in that work.

In this snapshot, we can find several hallmarks of a productive conversation. First, we can get a sense of how the principal wanted this conversation to feel to the teacher: casual and nonthreatening. He sought the teacher's permission, asking if he might drop by rather than telling her he would do so. The teacher did not seem surprised or concerned about the prospect of a visit from her principal, even on short notice.

Second, note that this principal approached the conversation in a personal and collegial way, not as a boss but as a friendly, yet focused, colleague. Soon, however, he got to the heart of the matter by asking the teacher to begin reflecting on the status of her differentiation efforts. He allowed her to choose the areas she wanted to talk about; mindful of the motivating factor of autonomy, perhaps, he stepped back to let the novice teacher control this part of the talk and provide the information that would be the focus of their conversation. Mr. Brooks led Ms. Peretti through discovery (thinking about the areas she wants to improve) and interpretation (what effects these practices have on her students), and by the end of the conversation, the two were in the midst of side-by-side idea generation that would result in Ms. Peretti's decision to try one or two new ideas as short-term goals. There is a hint of the cycle in progress when Mr. Brooks laid the groundwork for the next conversation, where presumably they would focus on her discovery of the new strategies, how well they worked, and what would be next for her. In a wonderfully simple, relationship-rich, results-focused way, this principal employed his conversation tool to lead differentiation, learn about individual and school progress, and assess this teacher's development in differentiation.

Mr. Brooks and Ms. Peretti's conversation provides a useful model. When we thoughtfully engage teachers in these brief conversations, we can gain important insights into the entire faculty's individual goals and concerns, and the problems they are having with the implementation of differentiation. Teacher by teacher and talk by talk, these conversations help us see what elements of leadership and management teachers need to move forward with their work. They support the development of a collective profile of where every teacher in the school is in the differentiation journey.

How Do Leaders for Differentiated Instruction Decide What to Talk About?

In the Northside Elementary case study, Principal Brooks encouraged Ms. Peretti to choose the differentiation content she wanted to discover and interpret, based on ideas that grew out of their conversation.

For many teachers, however, the broad range of topics along the differentiation spectrum may be so wide and deep that it's difficult to make a decision. And in many schools, the particular aspect of differentiation that staff are working on will be set by the yearly change plan and what it emphasizes for that year. Therefore, in many cases, it will be the operational vision for differentiation and the yearly change plan that provides the initial direction for leader–teacher conversations. As Danielson (2009) reminds us, "When consensus on such big ideas has been established, then it is understood that the implications of such ideas are always on the table for discussion; initiating a conversation on the intellectual rigor, for example, of a [differentiated] activity, does not constitute a 'gotcha' by the administrator. Rather, it simply reflects the faculty's consensus on the big ideas about learning that are the center-piece of all professional conversation and that an important implication of student engagement is intellectual rigor" (p. 46).

How Does a Leader Balance the Demands of Visions, Change Plans, and Individuals?

This is an appropriate place to recall that effective differentiation requires teachers to work with an understanding of five critical elements: learning environment, curriculum, assessment, instruction, and leading students and managing classroom routines. For teachers, understanding these elements and their interconnectedness, and applying the understandings in classroom practice are essential on two levels. First, these elements are the building blocks of meaningful teaching and learning in any classroom anywhere, and the power of differentiation will diminish to the degree that a teacher fails to understand and orchestrate the elements appropriately. Take out the word *differentiation* and substitute a myriad of other words (*collaboration, reading, interdisciplinary learning, process of science*—the list is very long), and this truth will hold. Therefore, to lead for effective differentiation is to help each teacher grow toward expertise in each of the elements *and* in the ability to incorporate the elements logically in his or her planning and instruction. This reality means that in some way—whether guided by the school's yearly change plan, selected by the teacher, or some combination of the two—productive conversations will generally need to focus on one (or more) of these five key elements. In a school moving toward differentiation, where the goal is to ensure maximum growth for each learner in the classroom, there are particular meanings attached to each of the five elements.

• **Learning environment.** It's good to have a generally or generically positive classroom, but if that environment feels less than invitational to a student with ineffective social skills, a student who cannot sit for long periods, a student who is bored because he or she already knows much of what the class is practicing, a student who is afraid of going home at night, a student with an off beat or highly creative view of the world, a student who feels stereotyped by race, and so on, then the environment is not yet supportive of every student's growth—and does not reflect the principles of differentiation.

• **Curriculum.** A teacher can be following a pacing guide, "covering" a list of standards, or moving through a text devotedly—and perhaps even with learning goals that are clear to students—but if that curriculum does not engage a portion of the class, or if it seems remote to the experiences of a number of students, or if it does not result in genuine understanding and ability to transfer what is "taught," then that curriculum does not reflect what is necessary for the teacher to differentiate effectively.

• **Assessment.** A teacher may administer and review the packaged "formative assessments" prescribed by a school or district, but if information gleaned from these does not relate to tomorrow's lesson, then the assessment results cannot be used to guide instructional planning; this is a nonnegotiable for effective differentiation. Likewise, if a teacher uses exit cards or writing prompts to monitor student learning but doesn't understand how to give meaningful feedback to students to help them develop greater agency in their own learning or doesn't understand how to seek patterns in student responses in order to adapt instructional plans, then the "formative assessment" is not formative in the way that it must be to support differentiation.

   • **Instruction.** If a teacher makes room in his or her plans for students to work in a variety of ways on a task, or to express learning differently, but does not regularly address students' varied points of readiness or development with learning goals, a central focus of differentiation is missing.

   • **Leading students and managing classroom routines.** If a teacher can clearly and accurately explain how to differentiate an upcoming lesson but doesn't know how to move away from "frontal control" in the classroom, it's unlikely that the teacher will execute the plans he or she can accurately explain. If "turning students loose" to work on two different tasks results in confusion and disorder, differentiation can't work. Rather, students need to understand the concepts of differentiation and be full participants in establishing and maintaining a classroom that works for everyone.

   The operational visions for differentiation's yearly change plans and productive conversations must address teacher proficiency with these five key classroom elements and ways in which they feed one another, and it must also address the particular ways in which the five elements should operate—individually and collectively—to support teacher attention to students' individual differences. A yearly change plan, however, may emphasize one or two of the five elements rather than all five simultaneously. In that case, leaders focusing on professional development must work with a "foreground and background" orientation. Although one or a few of the elements will be in the foreground of professional growth plans and conversations with teachers, it's essential that the other elements remain in the mix as well.

   So, for instance, if a change plan emphasizes work with formative assessment over a semester or the year, leaders and facilitators would provide information and support to deepen teacher understanding of the nature of assessment that informs teacher and student planning and how to use that kind of assessment in the classroom. At the same time, they would need to present the information on formative assessment in a way that makes clear its links with curriculum (e.g., aligning with KUDs, ensuring that assessments emphasize understanding so that all aspects of learning maintain a thinking focus, designing assessments that engage learners as curriculum should, and so on). Further, the professional development would need to acknowledge that strong assessment practices make the learning environment more positive for more students (e.g., students learn that making errors is safe in this place and will help them learn, and that understanding their progress will help them plan for future successes, which, in turn, nurtures a growth mindset). And, of course, the content would need to address the inextricable link between formative assessment and instructional practices. If a "formative assessment" does not result in instruction that works better for students, it simply doesn't qualify as formative. Therefore, these five elements of differentiation and how they appear in the operational vision as well as in a particular yearly change plan necessarily shape productive conversations.

The short version of our advice is that wise leaders will ensure ongoing conversations about all of the elements and the need for all five to function as a system, even in times when one of the elements might be in the foreground. But there is an additional layer of planning to consider: Any thinking, planning, conversing, and coaching for teacher development in differentiation must reflect the reality that different teachers will have markedly different profiles in understanding and applying the principles of differentiation. Each will see creating an inviting environment, providing powerful curriculum, using assessment to improve teaching and learning, delivering responsive instruction, and leading students and managing routines just a little differently and will make progress at a different pace. To be effective leaders, we must understand the big picture of differentiation as it's capsuled in an operational vision for differentiation, plan for current growth in aspects of the vision spotlighted in a yearly action plan, and engage in consistent background and foreground work to ensure that *all* teachers' knowledge, understanding, and skills develop in both big-picture and detailed ways. This means we have to reflect on where individual teachers are in a growth trajectory with regard to both vision and action. By doing so, we can differentiate for individuals within common goal sets. This level of planning is what we ask teachers to do in differentiated classrooms. Refer again to the Novice-to-Expert Continuum in Figure 1.2 (see p. 16), which provides some language for thinking about teacher development with differentiation. Figure 5.2 builds on that language to create a rubric that can more specifically guide conversations and planning for leaders and teachers. It is not intended to be exhaustive in its descriptions; it provides a starting

FIGURE 5.2

A Novice-to-Expert Rubric for Differentiation

 Download

Classroom Elements	Novice	Apprentice	Practitioner	Expert
Environment	☐ Flat affect ☐ Fixed mindset evident ☐ Low teacher–student connections ☐ Few meaningful student interactions ☐ Little student voice	☐ Student aware ☐ Growth mindset about more students ☐ General respect ☐ Some teacher–student connections ☐ Seeks some input from students	☐ Clear teacher emotional support for students ☐ Teacher growth mindset evident ☐ Sense of community ☐ High level of respect ☐ Sporadic student voice	☐ Full teacher–student partnership ☐ Teacher and student growth mindset evident ☐ Team of learners ☐ Learner- and learning-centered ☐ Consistent evidence of student voice
Curriculum	☐ Low goal clarity (no evident KUDs) ☐ Fact/skill-based, with low emphasis on thinking/understanding ☐ Low relevance ☐ Sticks to the script/text	☐ Greater goal clarity ☐ More thoughtful curriculum ☐ Sporadic engagement ☐ Occasional emphasis on understanding	☐ KUDs evident in planning ☐ Frequent planning for engagement and understanding ☐ Thinking often emphasized ☐ Time and support for meaning making sometimes built in	☐ KUDs clear to students ☐ High engagement for full range of students ☐ Understanding and thinking central ☐ Student voice incorporated into curriculum design ☐ Supports "teaching up"
Assessment	☐ Assessment of learning dominates ☐ Little/no use of formative assessment ☐ Grades emphasized over feedback ☐ Low alignment between KUDs and assessments ☐ Right-answer emphasis ☐ Repetition of facts and skills emphasized	☐ Some assessment for learning ☐ Use of formative assessment, but little evidence of resulting instructional change ☐ General alignment with KUDs ☐ Feedback is general/vague ☐ Growing emphasis on understanding	☐ Regular assessment for learning ☐ Good alignment with KUDs ☐ Understanding and thinking called for regularly ☐ Feedback emphasized over grades ☐ Some evidence of modification based on formative assessment information	☐ Assessment as learning ☐ Tight alignment with KUDs ☐ Actionable feedback ☐ Useful student-to-student feedback ☐ Regular evidence of instructional planning based on assessment information ☐ Student goal setting evident ☐ Differentiated assessments
Instruction	☐ One-size-fits-all/fixed, rigid ☐ Shows vague alignment with KUDs ☐ Teacher-centered ☐ Take-it-or leave-it approach ☐ Emphasizes rote learning, right answers ☐ Little instructional grouping or uses fixed groups	☐ Shows awareness of varied needs ☐ Provides some choice ☐ Uses largely reactive differentiation ☐ Shows general alignment with KUDs ☐ Calls for some thinking/understanding ☐ Shows more planning for interest/learning profile differences than readiness ☐ Features mostly low-prep differentiation strategies	☐ Features consistent, proactive, differentiation ☐ Shows good alignment with KUDs ☐ Attends to readiness, interest, learning profile ☐ Shows flexible use of some classroom elements ☐ Features respectful tasks ☐ Features some flexible grouping ☐ Incorporates some "teaching up"	☐ Regularly attends to readiness, interest, learning profile ☐ Is tightly aligned with KUDs ☐ Allows for student autonomy ☐ Allows for strong student voice in instructional design ☐ Features consistent use of flexible grouping ☐ Features consistent "teaching up"

Classroom Elements	Novice	Apprentice	Practitioner	Expert
Classroom Leadership and Management	☐ Rule-oriented ☐ Compliance-focused ☐ Teacher-directed ☐ Lockstep, tight ship, rigid ☐ Low trust of students ☐ "Manages" students	☐ Teacher-owned routines with some flexibility provided ☐ Incorporates some conversations with students about differentiation ☐ Some flexible use of time, materials, and space ☐ More evidence of teacher studying and responding to students ☐ Teacher still sometimes concerned with loss of control ☐ Uneven teaching of routines to support success	☐ Regular conversations with students about differentiation ☐ Teacher regularly seeks student input on routines ☐ Teacher uses many classroom elements flexibly ☐ Teacher balances need for flexibility with need for predictability ☐ Generally careful teaching of routines to support student success	☐ Differentiated instruction philosophy guides teacher's thinking and planning ☐ Evident trust of students ☐ Regular, rich conversations with students about differentiation ☐ Teacher leads students and manages routines ☐ Students partner with teacher to solve problems related to routines and processes ☐ High student ownership of learning

Note: Use this rubric to support reflection on, observation of, and conversation about differentiation.

point from which we can build descriptions that will chart group as well as individual growth. This rubric can also guide conversations that support teacher development in addressing learner variance.

What Are the Most Effective Ways to Lead Conversations That Support Change?

The "most effective way" to lead a conversation depends on a number of factors, including the teacher's level of trust in the leader and the value of the vision, the intent of the conversation, and the teacher's degree of expertise with the various aspects of the change initiative.

Then there's the fact that leaders tend to conduct conversations nested in our own personal leadership style. Do we favor a bureaucratic, command-and-control structure, or have we embraced the sharing of leadership across a learning community? Are we more comfortable with right answers or with inquiry? When it comes to accountability for learning, do we stress individual autonomy or collective responsibility? In daily practice, leadership behavior does not reside at one preferred point of these either/or dichotomies; it runs along a continuum. Still, all of us have a natural tendency to find comfortable spots on that continuum, and those preferred points have a direct bearing on how we talk with others. Refer to Figure 5.3's simple continuum of leadership preferences, adapted from the Learning Forward Texas Leadership Development Process training (Texas Leadership Center, 2014), and then consider this question: "Where do you most like to live in your leadership for differentiation?"

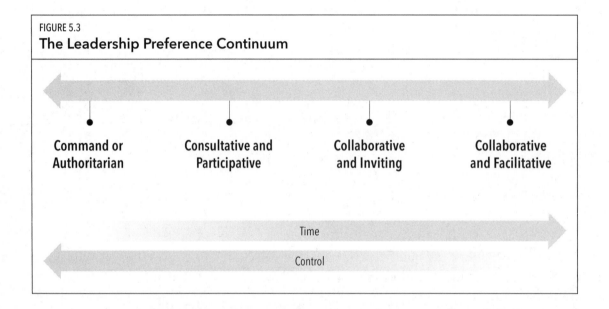

FIGURE 5.3
The Leadership Preference Continuum

A short explanation of the four "styles" can help leaders determine the part of the continuum to which they regularly gravitate. Many leaders attempt to lead efforts in differentiation by adopting a "follow me" style, leading the learning and dominating conversations by *telling*. The natural preference for this authoritarian style, the command approach, is efficient in terms of time and dominant in terms of control. Leaders who adopt a consultative or participative style still operate with the idea that their personal hunches about next steps in learning to differentiate effectively are sound, but they also believe in a more collaborative approach, inquiring about other ideas and methods before making the final decision on their own. The consultative leader is still firmly in control, although he or she seeks other ideas before deciding what the next move will be.

The other two styles in the figure represent more collaboration, less control, and more time expended in dialogue. The collaborative or inviting style seeks the opinions of others and believes in consensus to determine the next steps in leading schools to differentiated practices. The coaching and facilitative leadership style involves the most idea generation. This leader believes that the power is in the collective decision and that participants really know the best answer themselves.

The work of Walsh and Sattes (2010), which monitors leadership trends in education, suggests that in most cases, today's preferred leadership style is on the right-hand portion of the continuum. Personally, we believe all of us should carefully consider the factors that may influence how we lead conversations, and we feel that the style a leader adopts depends on how well that leader knows both *the context* of the conversation and *the person* with whom he or she is working. Therefore, there is no *right* way to lead these conversations. What matters is the leader's knowledge of his or her own preferred style and willingness to be fluid along the continuum, based on contextual factors and knowledge about the individual he or she wishes to engage in this talk. A useful admonition is, "Know your people and understand their culture" (Hargreaves & Fullan, 2012, p. 164). To this, we would add, "Know yourself, too."

At times, we may sense that a person needs some direction and thus adopt a command style in a discussion in an attempt to generate movement toward strengthening the teacher's differentiation skill set. At other times, we may sense that the most appropriate approach is the collaborative or coaching style, because the teacher needs acknowledgment of his or her efforts and demonstrates a willingness to be reflective during the talk. In other words, how we conduct a conversation depends on how well we understand the other person involved and what needs to be accomplished during this short exchange.

In our own practice, we have found that when in doubt about the appropriate approach to adopt during the conversation, it helps to simply ask! Consider what happened when Mike was coaching middle school teachers just a few years ago.

Mike was contracted to work in a middle school just south of a large metropolitan area. Ten teachers volunteered to have him in their classrooms for a minimum of four 45-minute observations, and these were followed by individual coaching conferences throughout the spring semester. One teacher in particular, a teacher with four years of experience who taught 8th grade social studies to a diverse set of students, taught Mike a valuable lesson.

Mike approached his duties gleefully, as he has learned to use a collaborative and facilitative coaching style, and he looked forward to using it with these teachers. After his second observation of the social studies teacher, he sat down with her for their first conversation. Mike launched into his best coaching talk, setting the stage, working to allow her to feel safe, and then exploring the work and her responses. He peppered the conversation with questions that were meant to both challenge her and support her.

After about 10 minutes of this conversation, the teacher leaned over, put her hand on Mike's arm, and quietly said, "Will you stop for a minute?" Trying to be mindful of her concerns, he did. "What's wrong?" Mike asked. "Is there something I left out?"

"No," she replied. "I just want you to stop coaching me for a minute. I *really* do not know what to do. You keep asking me questions, and I don't have answers. I really want to know what *you* would do. What are *your* ideas?"

This self-aware teacher provided a clear reminder that leading successful conversations depends on the leader's awareness of what's needed in the moment—and it depends on the teacher feeling safe enough to make his or her needs clear. This particular teacher was eager for and receptive to coaching, yet in a particular moment, she needed an approach that was *at least* consultative in order for that conversation to advance her growth. If Mike had asked her how she wanted this conversation to go and what kind of support she was looking for from him before he launched into it, he might have had a better idea of how to conduct it.

Reflect and Assess: How would you describe your preferred approach to conducting conversations? Command? Consultative? Collaborative? Facilitative? What examples from your experience provide evidence that this is the approach you generally use? How comfortable are you altering your style to better accommodate the other person and the context of the conversation? Can you think of a recent conversation about differentiation that would have developed more smoothly if you had been more fluid in your style? Map out a few scenarios of how the conversation might have gone if you had tried different styles.

How Can Questions Guide a Leader's Conversations?

During a useful conversation about differentiation, we are hoping that the teacher will discover and interpret information about his or her current practices and then, with input from us, decide on the next steps that will evolve his or her classroom practices. We and the teacher both want this conversation to feel collaborative, optimistic, and experimental. This outcome is more likely if we demonstrate genuine curiosity about what the teacher believes and what he or she thinks is the next stage of improvement in differentiated classroom practices. All of these goals and contextual benchmarks will be guided by our choice of questions, which will both prompt reflection and drive the talk.

Warren Berger (2014) reminds us that "good questioners tend to be aware of, and quite comfortable with, their own ignorance" (p. 16). He goes on to discuss questions as tools that not only open up thinking but also direct and focus it. There is a warning here for all of us as leaders of differentiation. Embracing questioning as a key strategy in conversations is one thing; questioning effectively and efficiently is quite another.

Most of us could benefit from refining our questioning skills. It could be that we tend to live in the command mode, a preference that diminishes the importance of the question and places more value on the declarative. The desire to see improvement can certainly tempt us to make position-controlled requests the centerpiece of conversations, but asking more and telling less is often a more promising approach.

Here are a few planning guidelines that can help create conversation-driving questions and practice asking them in relationship-rich, results-focused ways (Walsh & Sattes, 2010):

Guideline #1: Clarify the Purpose of the Conversation

Think through what you want to accomplish by asking a particular set of questions. In determining purpose, it's important to review the various "whats" that a great conversation about differentiation might focus on, discussed earlier in the chapter. Is your purpose (1) **information discovery**—to help the teacher explore an aspect of his or her differentiated practices; (2) **interpretation and speculation**—to invite the teacher to interpret successes and struggles to date; (3) **decision and action**—to help the teacher come to a decision about his or her next steps; or (4) **implementation and evolution**—to help the teacher commit to the action and ensure that the practice will become routine so the teacher will advance in knowledge and skill?

Guideline #2: Identify the Conversation's Focus

Think about what each question is asking and be sure you know why it's right to ask it. There should be total transparency in the focus for the conversation, negotiated either before the conversation or during it.

If you want to frame the focus based on the operational vision for differentiation or the year's change plan, the focus for content is prescriptive, reflecting the consensus decision about "what we want" or "what we are working on this year." In other instances, you may feel it wise to focus on the individual's growth and next steps.

Guideline #3: Select a Process

Think about how you want to pose your questions, in what setting, and under what conditions. How do you want the teacher to perceive the conversation? What will put the teacher at ease? Should you adopt a consultative style or a more collaborative and facilitative style?

Guideline #4: Word Questions Carefully

Use the purpose of each question to guide its wording but never forget that "words communicate content, but they also communicate information about the relationship between the speaker and the listener" (Walsh & Sattes, 2010, p. 17). You simply have to sure that the questions you will pose are clear in content and convey the intended tone—one that has been chosen with the person who will answer it in mind.

Over our years of working with a variety of school leaders, we have found the purpose-driven conversation framework outlined here to be very helpful for question generation. Here is a summary of useful questions for each of the four purposes.

Questions to Help the Person Discover Information
- What part of that lesson was successful?
- What are you noticing and why?
- What are your concerns about your work with _____?
- What are your thoughts on _____ and why?
- What do you still want to accomplish, and why did you pick that?
- How are you working toward _____? How much success are you having?
- What setbacks have you had with _____, and why do you think you have had them?
- What do you want to accomplish with _____, and why did you say that?

Questions to Help the Person Interpret Information
- Why do you think this is happening? What are the possible reasons?
- What did you notice when you changed _____?

• How different do you want the result to be? How will that be possible?

• If nothing changes, what will the result be? Can you live with that?

• What areas need to be worked on? Why did you choose those?

• Do you feel this is a weakness or a gap? Why?

• What is your theory of how to make the lesson stronger?

Questions to Help the Person Make a Decision or Move to Action

• What is your plan? Why is that the best plan for you?

• What part of the plan are you most excited about? Why?

• What steps will you take? What is your next step, and why is that the best step?

• Which direction do you feel most comfortable with?

• Which of the options that we have discussed do you believe would work best for you and have the best outcome?

• I'm interested in hearing which option will fit your needs.

Questions to Secure a Commitment to Implementation and Evolution

• What results do you expect? When do you expect them?

• How will you know you got the results you wanted?

• How will this change your work?

• What is the best way for you to get started?

• What is my part in this? How will you need my support?

• What resources do you need to kick this off?

• When do we want to get back together so I can see your results?

What Other Skill Is Necessary to Lead Productive Conversations?

Jim Knight, a well-known communication coach, advocates "partnership communication" and describes the skill of *listening* as integral to leading great conversations about schools and improvement. In a recent work, Knight (2011) clearly states the importance of listening in communication: "Almost any communication and leadership book identifies listening as essential. Nevertheless, authentic listening is a scarce commodity today. Our conversations at home, at work, and in the community are often more about jockeying for airtime than really communicating. Real communication is a two-way process, and for it to be authentic and humane, we need to take in at least as much as we put out. To be good communicators, we need to be good listeners" (p. 211).

Listening is how we demonstrate curiosity and the spirit of collaboration. It is also a way to explore possibilities and engage teachers in an open, honest conversation about the differentiated work. In a great conversation, the other person should be talking just as much if not more than the conversation's leader. This intentional refusal to dominate either the discussion or the decisions sends the teacher a clear message: your thinking is valued and needed just as much as that of the school's leader.

As we leaders develop our conversational skills and our questioning tool kit, we must also pay attention to the art and science of listening to ensure that differentiation ideas and concepts are explored deeply and meaningfully. Figure 5.4 highlights the qualities of mindful listening (Cheliotes & Reilly, 2010; Tschannen-Moran & Tschannen-Moran, 2010).

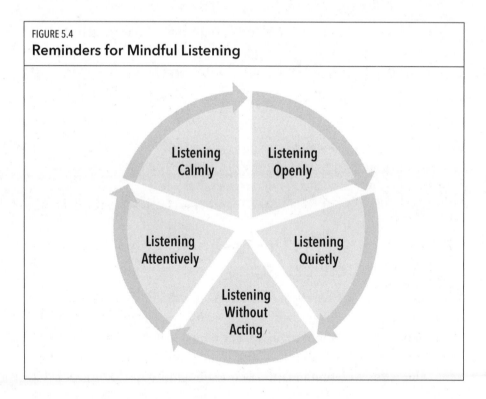

FIGURE 5.4
Reminders for Mindful Listening

What does it mean for a leader to exhibit these qualities of mindful listening during a leader–teacher conversation about differentiation?

• **Listening openly.** We must suspend judgment, jettison "right answers," and demonstrate curiosity about the teacher's ideas.

• **Listening quietly.** We must know when to stay silent, which communicates that we value the ideas the teacher is presenting. An excess of leader talk and idea generation actually diminishes the other person's sense that his or her ideas matter.

• **Listening without acting.** We must try not to jump in, "own the problem," and provide a solution. It's better to witness the teacher's thinking process and then draw the teacher's attention to appropriate solutions or strategies.

• **Listening attentively.** Rather than be distracted by other responsibilities or tasks, we must demonstrate to the teacher that this conversation is a top priority.

• **Listening calmly.** We must stay focused on solution finding and project a sense of joint efficacy in approaching differentiation dilemmas or opportunities.

In this chapter, we have covered a number of major concepts involved in leader–teacher conversations, and your impression at this point might be that rich, productive conversations are simply a matter of following the layered conversation protocol, fitting in the right questions, and refraining from talking at key moments during the conversation. Although these are *elements* of a productive conversation, what we know is that productive conversations involve a high level of skill from both the leader *and* the teacher. These skills must be learned and practiced by both parties. In fact, we believe that in strong schools, conversations reflect areas of focus and intentional work by leaders and the teachers who work with them.

While leading staff to focus on the content of differentiation and struggle together to cultivate differentiation that is robust and meaningful, we must also focus on how we communicate about differentiation. The conversation, then, becomes the most important daily tool for us to lead from the vision, learn from teachers about their current development, and assess schoolwide progress in this most responsive form of instruction.

Cultivating Leadership Competencies

Think about your status with the following concepts as you develop your efforts to implement differentiation. Which of these ideas require some additional thought or action on your part? What are your next steps in preparing yourself to lead great conversations about this important work?

❏ I plan conversations about differentiation that both reinforce relationships and focus on results from applications of differentiation.

❏ I conduct my conversations in a "side-by-side" manner, genuinely demonstrating a curious and collaborative tone.

❏ I gauge the content of my conversations based on where we are, and where the individual is, in implementing differentiation.

❏ I have a planned sequence for conversations and have definite contextual goals in mind before and during conversations.

❏ I am fluid in moving along the Leadership Preference Continuum (Figure 5.3), so I am reflectively paying attention to the best ways to support my conversation partners.

❏ I use questions to navigate through the conversations as well as to provoke thinking, action, and reflection.

❏ I exercise mindful listening as I talk with teachers about differentiation.

 Download

6

Testing the Soil to Determine If Differentiation Is Making a Difference

A large part of leading for change is accurately assessing the progress being made and communicating that progress to the teachers who are working so hard to make it happen. Often, however, we find that, as school leaders, we will champion a change to differentiation yet inadvertently neglect using the tools, strategies, and measures that would help us determine the degree to which change is taking place, the degree to which the change shows fidelity to a sound model, and the degree to which the change is making a positive difference for students and teachers. It follows that if we aren't regularly figuring out "how differentiation is going," we can't be communicating progress to teachers, and absent evidence of how well the work is actually going, the work likely will not go as well as it should. This futile cycle is typical in a frenzied environment that stresses action and overlooks both quality and product.

To compound the issue, we often feel compelled to approach "evaluation" of differentiation as a one-dimensional examination of student achievement, looking to local benchmarks or state test scores as the only measure of differentiation's impact—and impatiently examining these measures too soon. Then we, our supervisors, and our school boards become confused when outcomes are not all positive and practices do not seem to be uniformly effective. Here's a quick look into that dilemma.

"Is This Working? Are We Making Progress?"

Principal Vivian Walker is in her second year of leading focused efforts toward differentiation in her elementary school. During the first year of work, there was a lot of time and attention devoted to learning about differentiation, looking at student needs, establishing the purpose for differentiation, and creating an operational vision for differentiation. In addition, there was quite a bit of professional development for differentiation—almost all in the form of training early in the year and at the year's midpoint. Now, in the second year, Ms. Walker feels that her colleagues should have moved out of the initiation phase and into the implementation phase. She looks forward to making classroom visits and to seeing teachers put the principles and practices of differentiation into action.

What she finds in classrooms, though, is a mixed bag: wide variations in depth and quality of the differentiated practices. In her conversations with teachers, Ms. Walker also notices some pretty firm pockets of resistance. She really believes that the school should be further along overall, yet implementation is all over the map. Is their move to differentiation working, or isn't it? What should she do? Should she look to student test scores for evidence? Should she concentrate on individual growth? Should she look at the school as a whole and set standards for growth for all of her teachers?

This experience—and the resulting confusion—is common among those who are leading a differentiation initiative. The good news is that the unevenness characteristic of differentiation's early implementation is wholly predictable and usually temporary. Recall that when teachers begin to differentiate their instruction, they will choose pathways that make sense to each of them. The very nature of individual decision making will initially result in a wide range of efforts with variable results.

One way for leaders to steer a school past this is by seeking a better understanding of teacher thinking and practice, gauging progress, and communicating that progress. Knowing that growth is continuing, even if it is slow, can be the encouragement teachers need to maintain their efforts and keep the change moving forward. To do this, we can employ one of the most powerful tools in education: consistent formative assessment. The same basic process teachers in effective classrooms use to understand and guide each student's progress toward critical knowledge, understanding, and skills can be applied by a school leader not just to assess each teacher's progression in knowledge, understanding, and skills related to differentiation but also to discuss that progress, suggest midcourse corrections that will refine the teacher's work, and provide guiding support for the teacher's continuing growth. This chapter explores assessment processes that are appropriate at particular stages in a multiyear journey toward differentiation and offers suggestions about how to use those processes to inform steady, schoolwide progress toward deeply embedded differentiation.

Evaluating Progress: What Should We Do and Why?

In Chapter 1, we noted that teachers who effectively differentiate instruction continually monitor student growth relative to goals (KUDs), provide feedback to students, and make instructional changes based on information they derive from systematic interaction with students, classroom observation, and formative assessment practices. This emphasis on teacher goal clarity, knowing the results they are getting with students, and making responsive changes to their instruction is at the heart of differentiation. This process is no less essential to the success of leaders working toward differentiation.

When we think of exceptional instruction, one of the first characteristics that comes to mind is teachers looking at students in terms of each one's current status as a learner and then designing learning experiences that are just slightly "ahead" of that, thereby promoting growth within a structure of challenge and support. All leaders can employ this same approach when we work with individual teachers to implement differentiation and as we assess school progress in a holistic way. Doing this requires becoming proficient in both *assessing progress* and *evaluating growth.*

Tom Guskey (2000) describes *assessment* as "the appraisal of current status" (p. 47). He reminds us that formative assessment involves gathering information or evidence not to judge the merit or worth of an individual or idea but rather to clarify the current status of a project or initiative. *Evaluation*, on the other hand, involves a larger, more summative judgment of outcomes. Although assessment is certainly a part of evaluation, it is not a synonym for evaluation.

This distinction may seem like splitting hairs, but it's really quite important. Just as we expect teachers to employ frequent and targeted formative *assessment* in their classrooms to determine the current status of student learning (and, therefore, of teaching effectiveness), as leaders, we ought to gather regular, strategic, easily obtainable information to tell us the current status of teachers' translation of differentiation principles into classroom practice. Further, just as we expect teachers to use summative *evaluation* to benchmark each student's growth with the designated KUDs, we should routinely use more formal, evaluative measures to benchmark the overall impact of differentiation. In other words, we have to be concerned with both *assessment* and *evaluation* of the differentiation effort, and we must apply these processes at each phase of the change initiative: *initiation*—when teachers are learning about differentiation and getting ready to begin the change process; *implementation*—when teachers are applying the principles and practices of differentiation at increasing degrees of sophistication in the classroom; and *institutionalization*—when teachers are doing the work and continuing to make the work even better. In each phase, it's important that we take a three-tiered or "trifocal" view of progress, which means considering

• **The Near View:** How teachers are reacting emotionally to the press of change for differentiation, or their **affective response** to the change.

• **The Mid View:** How teachers are implementing the various elements of differentiation in their practice, or their **behavioral approach** to change.

• **The Far View:** How the school is **progressing as a whole** in its journey toward effective differentiation across all classrooms in the school.

We will look more closely at these three aspects in the pages ahead.

Do Leaders Assess Individual Growth Toward Differentiation or Whole-School Progress?

As a number of experts on school change have said, the answer to the question posed in the heading is "Yes!" (Hall, 1999; Hord & Roussin, 2013). Both individual growth and whole-school progress are essential to notice, and they influence each other in multiple ways.

Gene Hall (1999) uses the metaphor of an implementation bridge to think about change. This metaphor, expanded by Shirley Hord and Jim Roussin (2013), suggests that the bridge to the change we seek is filled with individuals, and that leaders must assess individual movement across the bridge in two dimensions. First, as leaders, we must continually assess the emotional (near view) and behavioral (mid view) responses each individual is having to the change. At the same time, we must keep track of how far across the bridge the group as a whole has progressed (far view). These frequent individual and group assessments should occur throughout the phases of change, and the data we generate on teachers' emotional and behavioral changes will be the first indicator that differentiation (and the bridge!) is taking hold. In short, the first changes that will emerge from the implementation of differentiation will be recognizable changes in the adults. These changes are the leading indicators that differentiation will begin to yield improvements in student learning.

This progression underscores why it's essential to develop and follow a systematic, logical plan to periodically assess the growth and depth of differentiation in practice, providing frequent formative and planning information as well as less frequent evaluative information that is focused on, but not restricted to, student achievement (Guskey, 2000). If the plan incorporates all three lenses of the trifocal view—near, mid, and far—we will have a steady flow of information to help us make frequent adjustments and corrections to the differentiation implementation plans. That information will also enable us to follow the effect of differentiation on student growth, teacher growth, teacher collaboration, parent satisfaction, and other important aspects of the kind of teaching that works better for more learners.

A useful framework for planning formative and summative assessment for an ambitious change initiative like differentiation was developed by Tom Guskey (2000), who built on Kirkpatrick's (1959) original model for judging the value of training programs. Guskey's five-level professional development evaluation model moves from simple to complex, and from "means" goals to "ends" goals. The framework offers a theory of how change for differentiation might happen, progressing from changes in reactions, to learning, to altering structures that support differentiation, to the application of practices at deep levels, and finally to significant student achievement benefits. It also provides insight and guidance as to how we can assess all three aspects of the trifocal view.

Take a look at Figure 6.1, which applies Guskey's Levels of Evaluation for Professional Development to the differentiation effort. Notice the logic behind the model—how the change made at each level scaffolds progress to the next set of changes. Imagine how these levels play out over time in the differentiation story, in all three phases of the life span of the change.

FIGURE 6.1

Guskey's Five Levels of Evaluation for Professional Development Applied to Differentiation

Evaluation Level	Questions to Ask	Notes
Level One: Participants' Reactions	• Are they excited about differentiation? • Do they think it will be useful? • Are they concerned about it?	It is important to assess reactions, but they only give an indication of the current satisfaction or lack of satisfaction with differentiation. Reactions are useful in determining improvements in the implementation plan.
Level Two: Participants' Learning	• Are they learning things they didn't know before? • Are they gaining skills they didn't have before?	It is valuable to gauge learning. The leader's theory is that if teachers are learning new knowledge and skills, they may be inclined to use them in the classroom.
Level Three: Organizational Support and Changes	• Has the school changed to support differentiation? • Is the climate becoming one of risk taking? • Are implementation problems being addressed?	Level Three assessment data are collected to determine how reactive the organization and classrooms are to the changes that differentiation will demand.
Level Four: Participants' Application of What Is Learned	• Did the participants begin to apply the new knowledge and skills?	This is the "golden turn" in implementation, when it is determined that it is appropriate to assess whether or not teachers are using what they have learned.
Level Five: Student Outcomes	• What is the impact on students? • Are students behaving differently as a result of the effort?	Level Five begins to measure "ends" goals—that is, the overall impact of the differentiation initiative.

Dig Deep: Review Guskey's Levels of Evaluation for Professional Development in Figure 6.1. How do you see each level relating to the near (emotional) view, the mid (behavioral) view, and the far (overall school progress) view? What levels of evaluation seem to have the greatest value in your school's differentiation journey?

Combining Levels of Evaluation with Initiation, Implementation, and Institutionalization

Guskey's levels provide a useful system for both planning differentiation and anticipating how the initiative will evolve over the differentiation initiative's life span, as organizational and classroom changes precede major changes in student achievement.

Just Beginning: The Initiation Phase

When teachers are in the "getting ready" phase of the work and substantial implementation is not yet a broad expectation, it makes sense to look to the first of Guskey's five levels of professional development evaluation, Level One: Participants' Reactions, for guidance.

Assessing reactions and emotional responses to change will give leaders an indication of how teachers are attempting to reconcile their perceptions of the changes they are expected to accomplish with their sense of how capable they are of meeting those demands. Because professional development that occurs at the beginning of the differentiation initiative may generate some strong opinions about the changes, insightful leaders will want to be aware of those opinions in order to help teachers work through them, even as they help teachers develop the knowledge, understanding, and skill that can lead to increased competence and confidence in differentiation.

There are many ways to assess emotional reactions to the change. These include but are not limited to surveys, exit tickets, focus groups, interviews, and personal logs. The questions used in these methods should focus on teachers' feelings and perceptions about differentiation, levels of excitement or apprehension, and anticipated benefits of the change. One extremely valuable way to assess perceptions and affective reactions is to focus on *the worries or concerns* teachers have as they consider what is expected from differentiation. We recommend using the Stages of Concern (Hall & Hord, 2001), described in Chapter 4 and illustrated in Figure 4.5, to assess teachers' reactions to differentiation. A relatively quick and effective way to gauge these concerns or worries is an approach commonly known as "the one-legged interview." Essentially, this is a one-on-one, very short (no longer than a person can stand on one leg), informal conversation between a leader and an individual teacher during which the teacher shares honest reactions about what he or she thinks is going on—and going wrong. The leader listens carefully without taking notes, paraphrasing and asking clarifying questions to get at the teacher's honest perceptions. There's a lot that can be learned in just one or two minutes. A question we like to use goes something like, "When you think about differentiation in this school and our plans to implement it, what are your concerns? What are you worried about?" Within Guskey's five-level framework, this is a Level One question, focusing on reactions and perceptions.

Conducted frequently, one-legged interviews allow the leader to sample teacher reactions all the way from the inception of the change through complete implementation of differentiation. It's important to note that the question's "negative wording" is intentional. This is a way to quickly move the teacher to describe his or her concerns. If we ask, "What is going well?" we're unlikely to get the kind of information necessary to gauge an emotional response. In addition, asking the question in the negative actually builds trust with the teacher, indicating an open, transparent attitude and genuine interest in learning about his or her perspective. The concerns or worries teachers express will probably fall into patterns, pointing the leader toward responses that will address the concerns and allow the teachers to move forward in their work. Recall Dr. Bennett, the high school principal spotlighted in Chapter 4. She was quite handy at assessing her teachers' reactions to differentiation, as illustrated when she asked them to list their worries about differentiation and turn those responses in to her as they left a meeting. Let's continue her story by checking in on her latest assessment efforts.

Dr. Bennett's One-Legged Interviews

Focusing on the first aspect of her trifocal approach to assessing differentiation progress, Dr. Bennett set a weekly goal of conducting 15–18 one-legged interviews. She met with teachers in the hallway, caught them in the workroom, and grabbed one or two minutes with those she saw in the main office. During each interview, she asked the same question: "When you think about what we are trying to accomplish with differentiation, and as you begin to implement the practices of differentiation in your classroom, what are you still worried about? What are your most pressing concerns?"

Through her conversations and probing, Dr. Bennett found that the majority of the teachers who had begun to use differentiation were concerned about having enough time to plan varied activities and worried that they were losing instructional time. In fact, about 80 percent of the comments were focused on this "management" stage of concern. Dr. Bennett realized two things: Teachers were definitely beginning to implement differentiation, and they were having trouble with the implementation. To Dr. Bennett, this was pretty great news, as it signaled that teachers were generally moving from *thinking about* differentiation to *actually using it* in a meaningful way. She reviewed the results of these interviews with her leadership team, and together they strategized solutions to address the teachers' management concerns.

Dr. Bennett used one-legged interviews to strategically assess progress in terms of how the teachers were reacting to the change while
making their first attempts at differentiation. During this initiation
phase, however, we will also want to get a sense of what people are
learning about differentiation (Level Two of the Guskey framework) and
what structural or organizational changes are occurring at the school
and classroom levels (Level Three) to support differentiated practices.
Remember, during the initiation phase, adults in the school will still
be learning what differentiation is, and they'll be doing this primarily
through professional development. During initiation, we have to operate
from the theory that if teachers are learning about differentiation and
their learning is positive, they will feel comfortable trying out the new
approaches in their classrooms. Assessing new learning about differentiation, then, is a useful early indicator of anticipated later results.

During the initiation phase, we want to begin determining if any
school or classroom structures are being altered to accommodate the
anticipated implementation of differentiated practices and better manage and support changes in teaching and learning. Are new schedules
being tried out? Is team planning time being expanded? Are changes
being made to resources and in resource distribution (Guskey, 2000)?
Combined with assessment of Level One reactions and Level Two
changes in learning, findings from assessment of Level Three structural
changes begin to coalesce into formative understanding of whether differentiation has a good chance of being implemented effectively and
deeply. In turn, insights from formative assessment suggest adjustments
we might make and suggest possible ways to deepen learning, reduce
anxiety, or support the change.

Figure 6.2 provides an overview of program assessment and evaluation approaches that are appropriate during the initiation phase.
Although the examples we've shared in this section focus on the very
beginning of change, it's beneficial to continue monitoring reactions
to the change, the availability of knowledge necessary to enable the
change, and structures that can support the change as teachers move
more deeply into the work.

Getting into the Work: Implementation Phase

The point at which many teachers are "crossing the bridge" to actually practice differentiation represents a great moment for the leader.
Conversations that were once solely focused on the purpose of differentiation and its elements now expand to include how to make it work

FIGURE 6.2

Program Assessment Strategies for the Initiation Phase

Targeted Level of Evaluation	Questions to Ask	Possible Strategies
Level One: Teachers' Reactions	• Are they excited about differentiation? • Do they think it will be useful? • Are they concerned about it?	• The one-legged interview to assess concerns or worries • Tickets out the door • Interviews • Focus groups
Level Two: Teachers' Learning	• Are they learning things they didn't know before? • Are they gaining skills they didn't have before?	• Pre- and post-surveys before and after training sessions • Interviews • Tickets out the door • Focus groups • Informal conversations
Level Three: Organizational Support and Changes	• Has the school changed to support differentiation? • Is the climate becoming one of risk taking? • Are teachers modifying their classroom structures to accommodate the changes? • Are implementation problems being addressed?	• Observation of changes in classrooms • Interviews with teachers • Focus groups • Surveys • Tickets out the door

effectively. Early on, during initiation, leaders may feel like theirs is the lone voice advocating for differentiation across the school. During implementation, however, we begin to sense that we have allies in our advocacy of the change.

Although troubleshooting any initiative, differentiation included, is fraught with challenges, it is actually music to the leader's ears when conversation shifts from "Yes, but _____" to "How do we _____?" This is resistance-focused talk changing to purposeful problem solving, as teachers stop explaining why differentiation won't work and instead try to figure out how to make it work. In addition, during implementation, we are actively building a second layer of change agents—teachers who constitute "a critical mass of [teacher] leaders led by the principal working on establishing a culture of ongoing learning" (Sharratt & Fullan, 2012, p. 173). Indeed, "achieving implementation can become so exciting that it blinds us to the truth that, in fact, implementation was not the goal of the change initiative, but rather a means to the goal of benefiting students" (Tomlinson et al., 2008, p. 109). Implementation is not the destination, but it is an important and encouraging stage in the journey.

During implementation, it is still instructive to regularly assess Levels One through Three measures (including conducting one-legged interviews to see how teachers' reactions to differentiation have changed), but we can find increasing benefit in looking also at Level Four and Level Five measures, which assess the *impact* of differentiation. Recall that as implementation progresses, it's a mistake to equate the effectiveness of the differentiation initiation with teachers doing something they call differentiation. The much better measure is the degree to which these teachers are working with fidelity to a sound model. Are they truly "owning," rather than "borrowing," the philosophy, principles, and practices that constitute differentiation? In this phase of change, our focus as leaders is to determine and study the range of differentiated practices in classrooms, from mechanical responses to practices that are sophisticated or refined and that signal intuitive, student-influenced teacher behaviors (Hall & Hord, 2001).

An obvious choice for measuring classroom practices (Level Four) is some form of classroom observation that supports collection of baseline data that can help us determine "to what degree [teacher] classrooms show key indicators of differentiation (e.g., teacher connections with students; learning environments that are both safe and challenging; a sense of classroom community; clear curriculum goals; ongoing assessment to inform instruction; attention to variance in student readiness, interests, and learning profiles; shared teacher/student responsibility for effective classroom observations, etc.)" (Tomlinson et al., 2008, p. 113). Observing differentiated practices in the classroom and documenting these baseline forms of data may require a specially designed walkthrough tool or instrument. In addition, we want to analyze state- or district-mandated observation tools (usually required for contract, advancement, or tenure purposes) to determine which particular aspects of the required tool address the aspects of differentiation that are the focus of the current year's change plan. For instance, it could be that, for a particular year of the change initiative, the focus of the change plan is development of teacher-created formative assessments that align tightly with KUDs and that teachers use to inform daily instructional planning. A transparent school leader would let teachers know that during regularly scheduled observations, he or she will pay particular attention to those indicators on the required evaluation instrument relating to formative assessment.

Remember that the intent of the implementation phase of change toward schoolwide differentiation is increasingly robust application of classroom practices and eventual examination of the effect differentiation has on students. As we use classroom observation tools to collect information about application of practices, we will therefore be paying particular attention to quality of implementation—from mechanical response to more sophisticated and meaningful practice. This focus represents a shift away from an emphasis on "reaction" assessment that was prevalent during the initiation phase to a "preponderance of evidence" focus that demonstrates how teachers are responding to the press for differentiation in terms of creating effectively differentiated classrooms. Of particular use at this juncture is the Novice-to-Expert Rubric for Differentiation (Figure 5.2) that sketches out the general direction of teacher growth in applying the principles and practices of differentiation. Although not intended as a formal classroom observation tool or checklist, the rubric provides useful guidance for ongoing, informal conversations as leaders engage teachers in thoughtful analysis of practice, which should, in turn, increase teacher clarity about the nature of effective differentiation. It is also helpful in understanding needs of individual teachers, groups of teachers, and the faculty as a whole for particular professional learning experiences.

A Few Strategies for Using the Differentiation Rubric During the Implementation Phase

• Use parts of the rubric to highlight one key aspect of differentiation during a faculty meeting. Show the range of approach for that key aspect, from novice to expert. Engage teachers in their own discussion of what they need to move forward in that aspect. Use this information to help teachers set goals for their own next steps and to establish midcourse support and direction.

• Feature the rubric in school-based professional development. Watch a video clip of a teacher differentiating in his or her classroom. Ask the teachers to watch the video and look for aspects of a key feature of the rubric. Debrief for implications in their own practice.

• When having short, one-on-one conversations with teachers, ask them to look at the rubric and show "where they are" in terms of their own classroom practice.

During implementation, analysis of "means" goals begins to shift more toward analysis of "ends" goals. In other words, as implementation progresses, habitual changes in teacher practices should become increasingly evident, with the positive effects on students becoming increasingly evident as well. This shift signals the need for a Level Five examination of student impact.

In essence, we move toward schoolwide differentiation to grow students in ways that are greatly expanded through attention to their varied readiness levels, interests, approaches to learning, cultures, languages, and so on. Level Five assessment is concerned with what many educators consider to be the ultimate goal of professional development—better student learning—and it focuses us on three categories of student outcomes (Guskey, 2000):

• Student **cognitive outcomes** include academic achievements such as knowledge, skills, abilities, and understandings. This category can reveal growth toward and beyond designated learning goals (KUDs).

• Student **affective outcomes** include attitudes, beliefs, feelings, or dispositions that students may develop as a result of differentiation implementation.

• Student **psychomotor outcomes** include how much more frequently students engage in class discussions, the quality of their participation in small-group tasks, behavioral outcomes such as improved discipline or attendance, more consistent completion of homework, and so on.

Student outcomes in these three categories can be collected through a variety of methods, and we will want to work with teachers to collect commonly understood cognitive measures such as standardized assessments, benchmark assessments, performance tasks, and portfolios, as well as teacher-generated evidence that can be particularly useful to spark teacher-to-teacher conversations about the progress individual students are making.

In sum, the implementation phase of the work provides fertile soil for assessing progress toward differentiation. Although the emphasis in the initiation phase was on teacher growth in knowledge, reactions to the change initiative, and organizational supports for the change, emphasis in the implementation phase moves to the "end game," including long-lasting changes in teacher behaviors and results with students. Continuing to use Level One, Two, and Three measures during implementation, the leader and leadership team add the Level Four and Five measures that explore with increasing depth the effect of differentiation on teacher practice and student outcomes. Employing tools such as the Novice-to-Expert Rubric for Differentiation and strategies such as aligning classroom observations and conversations with required evaluation formats, teachers and leaders examine the cognitive, affective, and psychomotor effects of differentiation on students.

The implementation phase *will* span years of concentrated, focused work. Its process is evolutionary before outcomes are revolutionary. The measures and strategies appropriate for assessment and evaluation in this phase (see Figure 6.3) must be used in a recursive fashion, generating snapshots of progress the school is making toward deep, embedded changes in practice that attends effectively to learner variance.

Deeply Embedded: Institutionalized Practices

The institutionalization of differentiation signals to the teachers, parents, and students that the principles and practices of differentiation have been successfully woven into the fabric of the school. This phase makes the message clear: "Differentiation is how we do business here."

Institutionalization, however, may present another challenge to the school leader. When the school is moving toward deeply embedded use of differentiation, there's a risk that teachers may perceive it as less of a priority, because there is less talk about the change. That perception can lead to a gradual erosion of resources, professional development support, and eventually implementation. We, therefore, must continue to be vigilant and focused on what needs to *continue* to happen to support differentiation even when the conversation around *differentiation as change* has ebbed.

In summary, institutionalization—the deeply embedded continuation of differentiation—depends on three factors:

• Differentiation being solidly rooted in the school through policy, revised vision statement, budget, schedules, and so on.

• Differentiation having generated a critical mass of "second-order change agents"—teachers who are highly skilled in and dedicated to its practice.

• Differentiation having provided for continuing assistance, such as ongoing professional development, a cadre of teachers to assist new teachers entering the school, and so on (Huberman & Miles, 1984).

Institutionalization necessitates that we continue to work with our leadership teams on these three elements. When many teachers have crossed the implementation bridge and are regularly teaching with attention to student differences at a high level of fidelity to the model (exemplifying expert descriptors on the Novice-to-Expert Rubric for

FIGURE 6.3

Program Assessment Strategies for the Implementation Phase

Targeted Level of Evaluation	Questions to Ask	Possible Strategies
Level One: Teachers' Reactions	• Are they still excited about differentiation? • Are they finding it useful? • What concerns do they still have about using it?	• The one-legged interview to assess concerns or worries • Tickets out the door • Interviews • Focus groups
Level Two: Teachers' Learning	• Are they learning things they didn't know before? • Are they gaining skills they didn't have before?	• Pre- and post-surveys before and after training sessions • Interviews • Tickets out the door • Focus groups • Informal conversations
Level Three: Organizational Support and Changes	• Has the school changed to support differentiation? • Is the climate supportive of risk taking? • Have teachers modified their classroom structures to accommodate differentiation? • Are implementation problems being addressed?	• Observation of changes in classrooms • Interviews with teachers • Focus groups • Surveys • Tickets out the door
Level Four: Teachers' Application of What Was Learned	• Have teachers begun to apply the new knowledge and skills? • To what degree are the teachers using the differentiated practices?	• Use of the Rubric for Differentiation • Classroom observation tools • Interviews • Surveys • Focus groups • Implementation logs • Teacher portfolios • Records of teacher team meetings
Level Five: Impact on Students	• What is the impact on students? • Are students behaving differently as a result of the effort? • What are other effects on students?	• Standardized tests • Benchmark tests • Teacher-created assessments • School records • Student portfolios • Student interviews • Student questionnaires • Student surveys

Differentiation in Figure 5.2), and the effects of these sophisticated practices are delivering positive student outcomes, our priorities shift to creating structures, resources, and support systems to ensure a long life for the practices.

Even during the institutionalization phase, we should continue to use measures from Levels One through Five of Guskey's framework.

Periodically and strategically, we will assess teachers' reactions to differentiation (Level One), even at this advanced stage. In addition, it will be important to see if teachers' more advanced implementation of differentiated practices continues to increase learning on their part (Level Two). As we look at policies, regulations, schedules, cultural aspects, professional development, and resources to support the sustaining of differentiation (Level Three), we can adjust all of these elements to address the needs of this stage.

As you will recall, Levels One through Three assess "means" goals. Institutionalization also demands periodic and probing looks at "ends"—how differentiation plays out in classrooms (Level Four) and various effects on students (Level Five). As differentiation becomes more and more a part of "the way we do things around here," it will become increasingly important to look at Level Four and Five measures over time, creating a long-term picture of how differentiation continues to shape outcomes for students and for teachers.

Putting School Assessment and Evaluation Together to Create the Scrapbook of Impact

"So, how is differentiation going in your school?"

Imagine your superintendent has just posed this question to you. It seems simple, but it requires a thoughtful response. In reality, what your superintendent wants to know can be summed up in four critical questions:

The Four Critical "How's It Going?" Questions for Differentiation

1. Where is differentiation in terms of initiation, implementation, or institutionalization?

2. How do you know?

3. What evidence have you collected to illustrate this?

4. What are you doing with what you have learned through the process of assessment to support increasing teacher proficiency with differentiation?

For differentiation to be deeply embedded in classroom practice, these are the questions we school leaders must ask ourselves over and over, as we continue to guide the "how" of differentiation. These four questions—which capture the essence of this chapter—must be what we and our leadership teams wonder as we work on a daily basis to implement differentiation across the school and troubleshoot the issues that arise in that process. The answers to these questions are not any simpler than the questions. To find them, we must gather and analyze the most appropriate information, gauging impact on teachers, the school, and students. Our discussion of "where we are" with differentiation must be continual, frequent, and illuminated with an ever-changing assortment of information.

In talking about assessment, Wiggins and McTighe (2005) caution that sound assessment practices result in collecting a scrapbook of evidence rather than one, two, or a few snapshots. We agree. If we are really serious about understanding growth toward differentiation and the effect differentiation is having on teachers, the school, and students, we will diligently, consistently, and persistently use the trifocal view to assess (1) teachers' affective responses to the change, (2) teachers' behavioral approaches to the change, and (3) movement of the school as a whole toward differentiation as core classroom practice.

Considering each of the three phases of the life span of a change initiative for differentiation (initiation, implementation, and institutionalization) in conjunction with guidance from Guskey's Levels of Evaluation for Professional Development can create a logical and systematic trifocal view of the change process to evaluate the eventual effect of differentiation. It helps us use what we are learning to adjust schoolwide differentiation plans and supports to ensure longevity of the practice and depth of its impact. The wise leader does not pay so much attention to the doing of implementation that he or she fails to notice if the doing is making a difference. Our experience leads us to conclude that sound formative assessment can actually be the catalyst for energizing movement toward quality differentiation, with positive results for learners and teachers alike.

Cultivating Leadership Competencies

Think about your status with the following concepts as you develop your efforts to implement differentiation. Wherever you are in the differentiation journey, take time to think about the progress you are making and generate plans to collect information to illustrate that progress.

❏ I understand and can explain the difference and varying roles of both assessment of school progress and evaluation of school progress.

❏ I use a reliable framework of evaluation to identify a theory of predicted changes and to assess progress toward those changes.

❏ I practice a trifocal approach to assessing the effects of differentiation on both adults and students.

❏ I use the Novice-to-Expert Rubric for Differentiation to focus on how teachers are applying the principles and practices of differentiation in their classrooms.

❏ I strategically use one-legged interviews with teachers to assess their emotional or affective reactions to the change and their approaches to the change.

 Download

7

Tending to Resistance That Pops Up

The January 1969 issue of the *Harvard Business Review* included an article called "How to Deal with Resistance to Change" (Lawrence, 1969). In terms of contemporary relevance, it could have been written yesterday. One of the most confounding problems the article explored and that still exists today is the seemingly illogical resistance that will arise in response to virtually any change effort.

The case for differentiation, as we outlined it in Chapter 1, seems anything but illogical. Differentiation is a way to meet some of the most pressing needs in today's schools. In subsequent chapters, we shared insights about how to lead differentiation. That work, for both leaders and teachers, can be challenging, but there is a methodology to it. And yet, as we've seen in school after school and district after district, even leaders who make a strong case for the "what" of differentiation and take steps to build the necessary knowledge about "how to do it" will meet with resistance.

The book called *How to Hug a Porcupine* (Ellis, 2009) uses humor to illustrate the real dilemmas that arise from teacher resistance. Ellis refers to the "human porcupines" in our lives, saying that "No matter where you encounter a porcupine, whether you are meeting him for the first time or have known her for years, having some reliable strategies in your back pocket can make all the difference in the world. With knowledge and the right attitude on your side, you can not only make the best out of a bad situation, but, with practice, learn how to avoid painful spots altogether" (p. 11). We agree. This chapter addresses resistance that predictably arises in response to a differentiation initiative. Although we cannot give a formula for making resistance vanish completely, we can, based on experience and knowledge, offer insights for anticipating and working with the resistance. Yes, resistance is probably inevitable—but fortunately, it is also manageable.

When Should Leaders for Differentiation Expect Resistance?

In Chapter 2, we detailed the life span of a differentiation initiative, from initiation (just beginning the work) to implementation (the "doing" of differentiation and getting really good at it) and institutionalization (ensuring its continuation and longevity). Although resistance can rear its head during any phase of the work, it often appears during the beginning implementation of the change. Resistance during this time generally does make sense. When a school is just starting to move toward differentiation, everyone is talking about it, professional development is focused on it, and there is a general energy around the topic, even for those who may have reservations about it. As implementation begins, however, teachers are figuring out how they will have to alter comfortable routines to incorporate the principles and practices of differentiation. At the same time they are being encouraged to take risks, they will likely encounter problems in moving ahead. In essence, the implementation dip we described earlier is a dip in confidence as it relates to differentiation. To put it simply, teachers may find that "the doing" of differentiation is harder than they expected, and leaders may indeed begin to encounter resistance to the general idea of differentiation as well as to the notion of sticking with it until the problems are resolved.

In the early days, resistance to implementation may be evident, for example, during the kinds of conversations we advocated in Chapters 5 and 6. Valuable one-legged conversations can help leaders understand the emotional responses teachers are having to the change. For instance, a teacher who explains his worries about differentiation to you in terms of the amount of time required for preparation and the toll it is taking on his personal life is signaling that if these issues are not resolved, he may not ever even attempt differentiated practices. In addition, as we engage teachers in conversations with the differentiation rubric (see Figure 5.2, pp. 98–99) in order to analyze where they are in the work, we may find that a particular teacher is still at the novice stage, even though the work is in its third year. Again, observation and conversation may, in fact, signal that the teacher is resistant to continued development as a sophisticated practitioner in the differentiated classroom. Continuous engagement with teachers will help leaders identify both individual concerns and patterns of concern across the faculty.

Consider the experience of Principal James Brooks, first introduced in Chapter 5, as he learns about pockets of resistance to differentiation.

Picking Up Hints of Developing Resistance

Northside Elementary School is in its second full year of work in differentiated instruction, and Mr. Brooks believes that the school is at the beginning of the implementation phase. He has established a culture of conversation at his school; therefore, it is not unusual for him to greet his teachers with "How is differentiation going?" and conduct a quick interview. It's clear to him that although many of his teachers are still very committed to the work, by November of the initiative's second full year, more than a few admit to having trouble with the management of differentiation—issues such as schedules, time, set up, materials, student movement issues, and monitoring student progress while students do different work.

This fall, three of the teachers that Mr. Brooks interviews are having serious trouble with the change. In his conversations with them, he learns that all three of them feel ill-prepared. They are not sure they can implement differentiation as expected, they explain, and they all express some degree of skepticism that differentiation will even really make a difference for their students.

While Mr. Brooks is pleased that only about a quarter of teachers he's interviewed are showing resistance to the change, he is also glad to know what their issues are and is convinced he can address them. He wants to help all teachers develop the competence and confidence they need in order to effectively address learner differences in their classrooms—and to feel a sense of pride and satisfaction in their work.

This scenario hints at the complexity of the dilemmas leaders face as they lead a change initiative for differentiation. Mr. Brooks's conversations revealed good news and bad news. The good news was that the majority of Northside's teachers were heavily into the work; the bad news was that some were struggling to the point of rejecting the change.

Although he knew resistance was predictable, he also knew he could do something to address the resistance he was starting to see. And in doing so, he knew he could make life better for the colleagues he values and for the students he and his colleagues serve.

What Do We Already Know About Resistance to Change?

To begin our exploration of resistance to differentiation, it is instructive to take a wide view of resistance to change and why it keeps us up at night, worrying about both the resistant individuals and our own leadership abilities. The first thing we know is that on-the-job change is complex; it has a technical component and a social component. Here is an explanation from that decades-old *Harvard Business Review* article that is no less accurate today than when it was written: "The *technical* aspect of the change is the making of measurable modification in the physical routines of the job. The *social* aspect of the change refers to the way those affected by it think it will alter their established relationships in the organization" (Lawrence, 1969, p. 4). Similarly, Powell and Kusuma-Powell (2015), two educators with a long experience steering the change process in schools, talk about an "adaptive aspect of change, one that calls for 'transformational learning' or learning that causes us to rethink our deeply held values, beliefs, assumptions, and even our professional ideality" (p. 67). These authors believe that the social aspect of change intertwines with other factors, making it often the more overwhelming obstacle.

The technical aspect of change and the complex social aspect of the same change can feed one another and fuel overt resistance. To illustrate, if teachers are going to implement differentiation in deep and sophisticated ways, they will have to develop new knowledge, skills, and understandings. Teachers who understand the logic behind differentiation may have little objection to or difficulty with the technical aspect of this change and the modifications it will require. But if these same teachers happen to be introduced to differentiation in a way they perceive to be threatening to their social standing or to the predictable social structure in the school, they may want no part of the initiative. It's the social aspect of the change that triggers resistance, even though the technical aspects did not. Here's an example from our experience.

The Technical and Social Aspects of Change Collide

Mountview Middle School generally exhibits a spirit of collaboration, strong personal relationships, and investment in ideas and joint problem solving. Teachers are encouraged to be reflective about their work and to pursue continuous improvement. Over time, Mountview has seen a shift in demographics and now serves a growing population of students for whom English is a second language as well as many students with special needs.

Principal Lee Ann Roberts is concerned that her school is losing ground in terms of responsiveness to its students and their diverse needs. She and her leadership team have researched differentiation, and they are convinced that a deep exploration of differentiation and long-term work to implement differentiated practices are part of the solution Mountview needs. Eager to move a change initiative ahead, they quickly put together a faculty meeting to launch the idea. There, Mrs. Roberts introduces the idea of differentiated instruction in carefully chosen words.

The reaction of Mountview's teachers is not the enthusiastic embrace the leadership team had expected. Many complain about the way the meeting was conducted, objecting to its tone—more like indoctrination or a sales pitch, they say, than the kind of exploration or conversation that is the norm within their collaborative culture. Others feel insulted. Is this move to differentiation an insinuation that they'd been "doing it wrong" all these years? That they don't care enough about their students now? That they aren't concerned with every child's success?

This brief look at Mountview highlights the relationship between the technical and social aspect of change. The teachers had confidence in their abilities and were used to enjoying a sense of autonomy in their work. The idea of a schoolwide move to differentiation, even if they saw the logic of it, signaled an uncomfortable change in the way teachers would behave with each other and (some thought) in the way the principal would relate to them. More significantly, it seemed as though the principal was, all of a sudden in this case, telling them how to do things "right." The perception that the basic processes and tone of the school were about to change, acquired during that one faculty meeting, continued to haunt Mountview for months and threatened to derail the differentiation initiative before it really began.

The example of Mountview reminds us that many of us treat a change like differentiation as though it were just a technical change. Powell and Kusuma-Powell (2015) point out that this approach can blind us to the reality that such a change may well trigger changes in the way faculty—and leaders—work, learn, and live together. The possibility that change will affect individuals' status within the organization is one of its most unsettling aspects. In a school moving to differentiation, teachers who have always been regarded as accomplished may now find themselves unsettled by the message that the techniques and practices they use are actually not so effective. This loss of status can cause additional disequilibrium in the school, sow the seeds of resistance, and erode collegiality. When teachers find the ground shifting beneath them in this way, it's natural for them to seek stability via the "way we've always done it."

The technical aspects of change can inspire resistance as well. A move to differentiated instruction requires teachers to develop new knowledge, understanding, and proficiencies. Those tackling this work should be encouraged to become experimental and take an approach that best suits their current level of knowledge, understanding, and skill. As they move more deeply into the work, it's certain they will discover additional gaps in preparedness, and each of these presents a challenge to the leader. If these preparedness issues are not anticipated and supported, teachers will see barriers where they should see opportunities for continued growth. What's worse, the technical side of the change can actually lead some teachers to retreat into a false sense of their ability to meet their students' needs. In the absence of growing proficiency with differentiation, it's easy for teachers to go into "I'm-already-doing-that mode" (Fullan, 2007).

As we have implied, successful change management requires careful attention to both the technical aspects of the change and the social aspects. Lawrence (1969) offers this perspective: "It may happen that there is some technical imperfection in the change that can be readily corrected. More than likely, it will turn out that the change is threatening and upsetting some of the established social arrangements for doing work. Whether the trouble is easy or difficult to correct, management will at least know what it is dealing with" (p. 8).

Is the Problem of Resistance Partially Our Own Fault?

Few of us are pleased to encounter resistance, yet we can and actually should learn a lot from it. Wise leaders move *toward* resistance and *into* it rather than distance themselves. They seek to understand the resistance so that they can create more effective support systems and the kind of environment that will build teacher competence, confidence, and collegiality. When things are not going well—and that will sometimes be the case—it is foolish not to listen carefully to the naysayers who are signaling trouble spots. Leaders who expect teachers to continually assess how learning is going and to adjust their teaching based on what the assessment shows them must apply this same principle to themselves as they lead change initiatives. This means continually assessing to see how teachers' learning about differentiation is going and adjusting development and support plans based on what the assessment reveals. Seeking the opinions of resisters and listening to their concerns provides valuable formative assessment of progress in accepting, understanding, and implementing differentiation. In turning away from dissatisfaction about differentiation, leaders may contribute to its demise in their school.

The tendency to ignore or quell resistance may be exacerbated if the person leading the initiation has a "fixed" mindset (Dweck, 2006). Those of us with a fixed mindset orientation may inhibit forward momentum for change in at least two ways. People with a fixed mindset tend to value "looking smart" more than actually learning. As leaders, we may feel that resisters' failure to embrace differentiation is a personal indictment—a criticism of our leadership. If we are fixed mindset leaders, we will not seek to understand teachers' misgivings because, frankly, we do not want to hear them.

Reflect and Assess: Consider your own approach to resistance and how your mindset influences your approach. Do you find that you generally move away from resistance or toward it? Do you have a quick, predictable reaction to resistance?

If we are leading for differentiation with a fixed mindset, there is a real danger that the goals of differentiation will be imposed on teachers rather than emerge from the teachers' collaborative learning and problem solving. Imposition of goals invites shallow thinking and shallow responses from teachers, necessitates that teachers respond to extrinsic goals rather than intrinsic ones, erodes teachers' sense of autonomy, and diminishes long-term commitment to the work (Pink, 2009). Ironically, forcing teachers to maintain a focus on imposed goals will, in fact, *perpetuate* resistance. As Kerry Patterson and his co-authors put it in the book *Crucial Accountability*, "Raw power, painfully applied, may move bodies, it may even get people to act in new ways, but it rarely moves hearts and minds" (Patterson et al., 2013, p. 110). Under better circumstances, the hearts and minds of teachers will be moved as their understanding of differentiation deepens and they have the opportunity to see the positive effect it has on their students. A leader's trigger response to apply his or her position of power to force teachers to begin using differentiated strategies will almost always have negative consequences. "Every time we decide to use our power to influence others, particularly if we're gleeful and hasty, we damage the relationship" (Patterson et al., 2013, p. 114). Although it may be second nature (and feel most efficient) for us to try to force the change, force kills collegiality and can actually strengthen resistance. Any success it brings will be short-term at best. See Figure 7.1 for a summary of various ways a leader can unintentionally contribute to resistance.

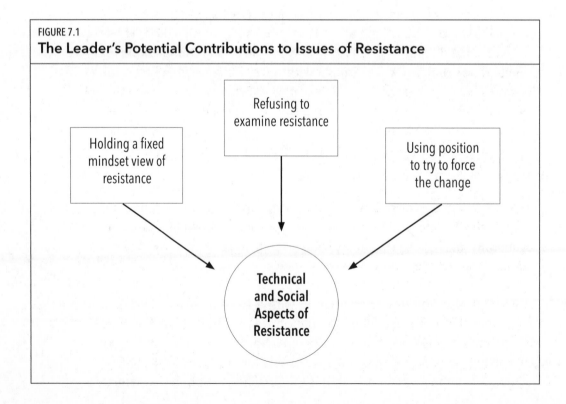

FIGURE 7.1
The Leader's Potential Contributions to Issues of Resistance

Refusing to examine resistance

Holding a fixed mindset view of resistance

Using position to try to force the change

Technical and Social Aspects of Resistance

Are Impatience and Speed Sabotaging the Work?

Beyond the human inclination to avoid the unpleasant and a fixed mindset orientation, there is another possible leader-generated cause of resistance. The plans the leader has made for implementation may not have taken into account teachers' varied paces of learning.

In Chapter 4, we built the case for the gradual release of responsibility framework for learning (Pearson & Gallagher, 1983) as it applies to adults as well as children. In this model, learners move from maximum support ("Let me tell you about this and show you what it is") to shared attempts and interactions ("Let's work on this together for a while") to guided support ("Now you try it without much of my help") and finally to independent practice and competence ("You do it and continue to do it"). Because teachers learning about differentiation will progress through these stages at varied rates, resistance to differentiation may appear when the gradual release of responsibility is not gradual enough for some teachers. Oftentimes, it crops up when teachers feel they have been asked to move too quickly to independent practice without having received the proper support in the "We do" and "You try" stages (Murphy, 2014). Simply put, a big change such as movement toward differentiated instruction tends to begin with a lot of training at the first stage ("Let me show you"), and then we expect teachers to navigate themselves through the second and third stages (doing it together and trying out strategies) with little strategic or systematic support or help. In essence, in many failed differentiation initiatives, we move directly from Stage 1's "Let me show you" to Stage 4's "Now you do it." Our failure to understand and use a model such as the gradual release of responsibility in planning professional development can contribute to the resistance to and premature demise of the work. Consider this example.

The Best-Laid Plans of Wallace County Schools

The Wallace County School District invested in differentiated instruction to dramatically alter the way teachers were teaching reading in the elementary grades and positively affect students in terms of their reading proficiency. Part of the district's work was to develop a central vision for differentiated reading instruction. Within a few months of the first year of the districtwide differentiation initiative, Wallace County Schools had generated a powerful district vision statement.

By early spring, teachers and principals were immersed in highly orchestrated training about differentiation and its critical elements, which extended throughout the rest of the school year. That summer, principals and their leadership teams met with external consultants to plan how they would support differentiation in their schools in the initiative's second year.

These external consultants began their work with each leadership team by showing them what components to include in their plans, why it was so critical to formulate a strategic plan, and how the leadership team could manage the plan. Then, as a "homework assignment," each leadership team was charged with drafting a plan for their school, which would be reviewed in the next round of training, scheduled for October. In essence, each leadership team had about three months to create their draft plans. To the external consultants' dismay, when the training began in October, only 3 of the 11 elementary schools had *any* plan to share.

In Wallace County, there may have been many contributing factors to the lack of tangible plans. The district leadership may have sabotaged the effort by overloading school principals with work, or school principals may have given higher priority to work other than construction of the plan. But when looking at this scenario through a gradual release of responsibility lens, it also appears that during the summer, the external consultants may have done a great job in "showing" the teams how to design and plan but provided no assistance to the teams in beginning to design their plans or creating a mock plan together. In spite of good intentions, the design of the work *led* to the resistance that was exhibited in October. The eight teams who produced nothing had not intended to be resistant. In fact, they created nothing because they were less than confident in creating the plan. They were thrust too quickly from "Let me show you" to "Now you do it." It's very possible those same leaders may reproduce the error for their teachers by providing early "Let us show you" staff development and then progressing almost immediately to "Now you do it."

How Can Resistance to Differentiation Be Managed?

The question now shifts from "What do leaders need to understand about the issue of resistance?" to "What do leaders *do* about it?" In many schools, resistance is evident, and it may have taken hold because of technical or social aspects of the change process, through fixed mind-set responses to change on the leader's part, or because the design for change moved teachers too quickly from "training" to full expectation for independent performance. Whatever the reason, some teachers may have become attached to underperformance and a natural immunity to change (Kegan & Lahey, 2009). By predicting resistance and then managing it, the leader is designing ways to shift inertia—deeply cultivating teachers who, with effective support, make dramatic moves to differentiation, eventually resulting in self-sustaining classroom practice (Tschannen-Moran, 2004).

The ideas that follow are not *solutions* to resistance but rather useful guidelines leaders can use to reflect on how they might approach and address resistance in a relationship-rich, results-focused way.

Guideline #1: Change the Way You Think About Resistance

Understand that change is not easy. When you, as a school leader, ask teachers to markedly alter their practice, always remember that you're asking them to do so while a great number of young people are moving around them, needing their steady and focused attention. Further, teachers have lives outside of school that demand and merit their attention and energy (Evans, 2001). In a significant and sustained change effort, things are likely to get tense sometimes. Accept it as an opportunity to be aware of and learn from the tension in order to provide better leadership and support better outcomes. Move toward resistance, not away from it. Honor the feelings of the people whom you ask to do the work of change. See resistance as a vehicle for helping you smooth the way to change, not as a threat to your leadership.

Guideline #2: Ask About the Problems People Are Having

From the outset of the change process, make it a point to ask how people are feeling about the change. Use one-legged interviews as a tool to begin conversations about their perspectives. When you ask, "How is differentiation going in your classroom? or "What are you worried about?" you are actually uncovering roadblocks and issues that will hold people back unless you can address them. By proactively asking people for their perspectives, reacting positively and with gratitude when they share, and then addressing their concerns, you build trust and collegiality. You become a partner in change rather than an issuer of mandates. As you move into resistance rather than away from it, you model risk taking, and more to the point, you model trust in the wisdom of the people whom you seek to lead. You model the same growth mindset message you want teachers to use in their classrooms: "Of course this is hard, but we can do hard things. We'll figure it out together, and we will grow."

Guideline #3: Don't Force the Issue

If you realize you're issuing mandates or feel like you're imposing your ideas on colleagues, it's a good time to stop, reflect, and find an alternative approach. Resistance is typically a sign of insecurity or uncertainty on the resister's part. Instead of arguing or commanding in the face of resistance, remember that the leader's job is to build competence and confidence that will lead to greater autonomy and personal satisfaction in a teacher's work. What a teacher (perhaps rightly) perceives to be negative or even alienating responses from a leader is highly unlikely to result in positive behavior from the teacher. Instead, ask yourself, "What actions can I take—and guide others to take—that will replace a teacher's reluctance with purpose and a sense of possibility?" See Figure 7.2 for a synopsis of alternatives to the use of force to create the desired change (Patterson et al., 2013).

FIGURE 7.2

Alternates to Using Force When Changing Resistant Practices

Alternative Strategy	Specific Actions	What It Sounds Like
Connect short-term benefits with long-term pain	Show how the short-term actions the teacher is demonstrating are actually going to connect to long-term problems or outcomes.	"I can see that you believe the move to differentiation takes a lot of extra planning. I'm worry, though, that if you do not begin to incorporate differentiation into your planning, you will become isolated from your other teammates and will have little to contribute to team planning."
Introduce the hidden victims	Describe the unintended and invisible effects an action is having on others.	"We need to talk about how your unwillingness to use differentiation is having an impact on not only your teammates but the parents and students you serve as well."
Hold up the mirror	State how the teacher's actions are being viewed by others.	"Here is what I am seeing. It is beginning to look like you do not care about being a member of your team or part of this work."
Connect to existing rewards	Describe how the work in differentiation would benefit them.	"It seems to me that as a team leader and someone who has a lot to contribute to our school's success, you would benefit from becoming a leader in differentiation rather than an enemy of it."

What Are Some Other Strategies for Managing Resistance?

The previous resistance guidelines invite the school leader to determine first whether or not his or her mindset and reaction to resistance might be at least contributors to resistance. Following are *management* strategies that need to be deeply embedded in daily planning for and management of full implementation of differentiation.

Strategy #1: Use a Change Formula

We recommend using the following "change formula" to manage resistance:

$$D \times V \times F > R$$

Dick Beckhard and Reuben Harris (1987) popularized this simple yet effective management formula for leaders who encounter resistance. As adapted slightly to relate to the subject at hand,

D = The amount of dissatisfaction teachers feel about the status quo.
V = The vision for differentiation and how it will affect teachers and students.
F = The first steps to begin working toward that vision.
R = The amount of resistance that is put forth.

In the Beckhard and Harris model, the product of D, V, and F must be greater than the amount of resistance that people will naturally feel about the amount of labor necessary to make the change—initiating, implementing, and institutionalizing differentiation—work.

You can use this formula informally as you think through conversations you are having with individuals or the faculty as a whole in order to minimize the likelihood of resistance. For example, early in the initiation phase of change, leaders will need to (1) create an urgency for the change through clarifying problems with the current status of classroom instruction, (2) ensure that staff members understand what they are trying to accomplish (the vision), and (3) collaboratively develop short-term steps to get started (Murphy, 2014).

Consider the following case study of a principal who orchestrated specific changes in his school's mathematics instruction (Murphy, 2014). Although it focuses on one facet of differentiated instruction, it serves as an excellent example of how Beckhard and Harris's change formula can help a leader manage resistance.

$D \times V \times F > R$ in Action

Bill Reynolds is a third-year principal in a rural K–5 school. He prides himself on understanding his staff members and knows that the quality of instruction in mathematics must improve quickly. After numerous visits to classrooms and discussions with his teachers, Mr. Reynolds begins to recognize that assessing and grouping students in smaller instructional groups based on need may lead to more accurate, timely, and focused math instruction. However, he also recognizes that many of his teachers like their current form of whole-group math instruction and believe it is the best and most efficient way for them to "cover their content."

Mr. Reynolds uses the $D \times V \times F > R$ formula to plan conversations with his staff members to accelerate change and, at the same time, reduce possible resistance to the instructional shift. Here are his personal planning notes to manage possible resistance to this way of teaching math:

D = Need to raise the current level of **dissatisfaction** with the current way of teaching math in whole group. *Action plan:* Begin sharing data in small grade-level teams and sharing the best, most practical research on differentiation and how a differentiated approach may help align small-group instruction with targeted, tailored instruction.

V = Need to clarify the **vision** for what we are trying to create. *Action plan:* Make sure I can clearly describe what we are hoping to see in classrooms and use that language every time I'm with groups talking about mathematics.

F = Need to take the **first steps** toward the change. *Action plan:* Describe my requests, and break down the vision into manageable first steps that are individualized, based on personal comfort levels. During small meetings, ask, "What would your first steps be?" and then follow up with each teacher on his or her response.

Strategy #2: Leverage the Factors That Affect Full Implementation

Fullan (2007) describes four factors that affect "the extent to which teachers [and students] alter their practices, beliefs, use of new materials, and corresponding learning outcomes in the direction of some sought-after change" (p. 86). Recall that resistance often appears during implementation rather than during the initiation stage of the work. Although we have explored these four factors that influence implementation in Chapter 2 and Figure 2.3, they deserve a second screening here as we discuss resistance. It makes sense to remember and use these factors on a continual basis as you manage implementation. Doing so effectively reduces resistance.

Need. Differentiation must continue to be viewed as addressing priority needs in the school. Often, teachers will view differentiation as a *logical* answer to their instructional and learning issues, but how that plays out in practice may not become entirely clear until well into implementation. The perception must continue to be that differentiation is addressing real needs and that teachers are making progress toward making it happen (Fullan, 2007).

Clarity. To combat issues of resistance, it is essential that teachers implementing differentiation are clear on what they are supposed to be doing differently. Differentiation is worth the work, but as is the case with most substantial change, it is not a quick and simple solution. Many teachers involved in large-scale initiatives cannot describe the essential features of the innovation they are using, and the greater the complexity of the reform, the more likely it is that clarity will be an issue (Fullan, 2007). For this reason, leaders must constantly attend to issues of clarity and work to understand teachers' perceptions of what differentiation is and what is being asked of them in terms of operational changes in their classrooms.

Complexity. Related to the factor of clarity, complexity addresses the "difficulty and extent of change required of the individuals responsible for implementation" (Fullan, 2007, p. 90). Changes likely to bring about pervasively more positive results are typically complex, so while complexity creates challenges for implementation, it should also result in greater benefits. Leaders are cautioned to be cognizant of the complexities of implementing differentiation and break it down into components that build on each other as teachers become more and more sophisticated in their knowledge, understanding, and skill.

Quality and Practicality. A change plan for differentiation and communication about it must be rooted in quality of the ideas and quality of implementation. That is, teachers must come to understand the change as having real, tangible benefits and usefulness to them and to their students. At first, they may view differentiation as being "something more," which isn't illustrative of a practical solution to their teaching and learning dilemmas. Therefore, leaders must make it a priority to help teachers see the connections between their real-world teaching issues and the changes differentiation asks of them.

Strategy #3: Use Gap Conversations

Patterson and his fellow authors describe a *gap* as a space between expected performance and observed performance—"serious, consequential, and complex deviation, something that might be hard or even risky to discuss" (Patterson et al., 2013, p. 77). In Chapter 5, we described conversation frameworks that can engage teachers in collaborative conversations about differentiation and what is happening in their classrooms (see pp. 103–105 and Figure 5.1). These conversation frameworks are useful in creating rich relationships and enhancing focus on the work. Although we believe conversations with all teachers should generally focus on those two goals, we also believe that with resistant teachers, when all else fails, we may need to have a very difficult, uncomfortable, and likely challenging *gap conversation* (Patterson et al., 2013). The following framework, adapted from the work of Patterson and his co-authors, lays out the steps for this conversation and provides important guidance for leaders who find themselves in need of using a form of accountability talk with resisters:

How to Conduct the "Gap Conversation" to Reduce Resistance
- Make it safe to address the topic by creating the best setting and context possible.
  - Describe the conversation and the goals for it.
  - Describe the gap that exists between the expected practice and actual practice.
  - Share the gap's impact on students, adults in the school, and the organization as a whole.
  - Explore the gap with genuine curiosity, and avoid judging.
  - Develop new versions of practice to address the gap and compare them with one another.
  - Agree on the plan to close the gap, and commit to action.

When using this framework, you will want to begin the conversation with ideas of mutual respect and shared purpose. As the conversation progresses and you begin to describe the gap or the discrepancy between what a person is expected to do and what it appears that person is actually doing, it's best to be direct. "Don't play games; merely describe the gap. Describing what was expected versus what was observed is clear and simple, and it helps you get off on the right foot" (Patterson et al., 2013, p. 81). In this case, keep the focus on the gap that exists between the operational vision for differentiation, the goals for the year, and the teacher's current behavior. Honestly invite the resistant teacher to explore the gap with you, and talk frankly about his or her issues in implementation. Many of us will view this as an invitation for excuses, but the fact is, the framework allows for that. What we're really doing is allowing the teacher to *explain* and inviting him or her to be a part of a genuine exploratory conversation.

The next step in the sequential framework is to ask the teacher to build a version of changed behavior that would reduce the gap. At this point, accountability for differentiation comes front and center. The teacher is now respectfully required to talk about how he or she could reduce the gap and make significant progress in implementing differentiated instruction. At this juncture, you will want to exercise the best forms of responsive listening and probe to learn all you can about the teacher's ideas.

After you've listened to and learned about the teacher's plan, it's time to build your own version of an effective plan to address the gap. This building portion of the gap conversation is powerful because it allows both parties to essentially create versions of how differentiation might begin to look in the teacher's classroom, compare ideas, and come to a compromise about next steps.

If you conduct the gap conversation mindfully, you can actually build your relationship with a resistant teacher by holding him or her accountable for movement toward differentiated practices. If mutual respect and mutual purpose can be maintained throughout the conversation, it's likely that the two of you will actually leave the conversation feeling more connected to one another and having greater clarity about what will follow.

Although this chapter has focused on resistance specifically, in reality, Chapters 2–6 are about reducing resistance as well. If leaders collaboratively develop a vision for differentiation; devise yearly change plans to break the work into definable chunks; design professional development that perpetuates the momentum for developing knowledge, understanding, and skill about differentiation; engage teachers in deep conversations about differentiation; and construct motivating ways to assess and celebrate progress, they are well on their way to minimizing reluctance or resistance to the work. Nonetheless, some degree of resistance will appear at some point and can be perceived as being dangerous to the continued implementation of differentiation.

We believe that resistance usually happens for a reason. Sometimes a leader's mindset creates resistance or the way a leader responds to resistance exacerbates it. Sometimes teachers who are reluctant to implement differentiation react negatively because there has been inadequate support to help them make the change. In other words, it's not necessarily differentiation itself that's the primary catalyst for resistance but *how the plan to bring about schoolwide differentiation is being implemented.*

To that end, we stress again that resistance is something a leader can tend to—can both predict and manage. As Lawrence (1969) says, "When resistance does appear, it should not be thought of as something to be overcome. Instead, it can best be thought of as a useful red flag—a signal that something is going wrong. To use a rough analogy, signs of resistance in a social organization are useful in the same way that pain is useful to the body as a signal that some bodily functions are getting out of adjustment" (p. 8). Use the checklist that follows to reflect on your status relative to some key tools, concepts, and actions that can support leaders in predicting and managing the resistance to change.

Cultivating Leadership Competencies

Consider the following competencies that are crucial for managing resistance to differentiation. Which do you need to learn more about or develop? What other steps could you take to better predict and manage resistance in your school?

❏ I can identify the signs of resistance in my school.

❏ I understand and can analyze the technical and social aspects of resistance.

❏ I use the gradual release of responsibility framework to guide professional development planning, attending to the underlying needs of teachers and heading off resistance.

❏ I practice a fluid or growth mindset toward differentiation.

❏ I use Beckhard and Harris's Change Formula to plan for implementation of differentiation.

❏ I can engage a highly resistant teacher in a highly effective gap conversation.

 Download

Conclusion: A Call to Lead for Lasting Growth

In the United States, a nation rooted in the assertion that all people are created equal, school leaders and teachers have often struggled with how to address the obvious student variance that comes into the classroom daily. It would seem that the appropriate goal is to ensure that students, regardless of class, ethnicity, culture, experiences, family support, and a range of other descriptors, have access to the richest, most compelling learning experiences a school knows how to develop. Then, it seems we'd want to build the scaffolding necessary to support success with that opportunity for a very broad range of learners.

In reality, there are three ways we can group and teach with student differences in mind. The option we choose is of great consequence. First, we can place all kinds of learners in a room together and teach them as though they were all the same. While we regularly do that, most of us are keenly aware that the approach drives many students to perpetual discouragement and consigns others to perpetual boredom. In both instances, satisfaction that should stem from learning is extinguished, and the will to do the hard work of learning diminishes until it disappears all together.

Second, we can try to figure out (which we do very poorly) who is smart, who is average, and who is not smart, sorting them into classrooms based on what we perceive to be their capacity to learn. This approach, which is evident in most schools, becomes a self-fulfilling prophecy on multiple levels. Not only do students whom we label as "deficient" or "average" feel those labels at the core of their being, but the feelings are multiplied by the realities that their classes are frequently taught by less prepared or less enthusiastic teachers who teach a curriculum that is flat, uninspired, and repetition-based, and their classmates are rarely energized to lift the level of conversation. Students whom we label as "smart" too often develop limited understanding of and appreciation for people whose backgrounds differ from their own, learn to learn for reward rather than for the intrinsic pleasure that should derive from understanding the world around us, develop a sense of entitlement, and live with a kind of competitive pressure to be the best that damps the opportunity to experience youth.

The third option is one we've tried less often. We can create heterogeneous classrooms and attend to students' varied learning needs in the context of rich and rigorous curriculum designed to engage a broad spectrum of learners, with scaffolding in place to assist students in moving steadily toward—and beyond—shared goals. This third option—differentiating instruction in mixed-readiness classrooms—is what we advocate in this book. While it has been tried less often than the other two options, when it has been implemented well, the results have been quite positive. (See, for example, Burris & Garrity, 2008; Tomlinson et al., 2008.) Moving to effective differentiation is both challenging (as is all change) and doable. A case in point follows.

Just as we were completing the manuscript for this book, *Education Week* (2015) announced its annual list of "Leaders to Learn From." Each of the spotlighted leaders was impressive because of his or her dedication to a vision and capacity to enlist the energies of others in helping to achieve that vision. One of the awardees was particularly striking to us both because the vision he pursued aligns so well with the vision we've commended for differentiation, and because the brief profile (Ujifusa, 2015) that accompanied the award mirrored the principles of leadership for change that the two of us believe in and have shared in this book.

William H. Johnson is superintendent of the Rockville Centre Union Free School District in Rockville Centre, New York. In his 29 years in that job, he has worked from a central vision that drives all of his work. In the *Education Week* profile, he's quoted as saying he believes his job is not to discover a child's limits, but to give children ways of breaking those limits. Johnson's brother was born with severe physical disabilities and struggled with the stigma that accompanied him to school. Having seen his brother overcome that stigma to be an accepted member of his community with a successful career, Johnson set a goal of giving every child the chance to become something wonderful because, he believes, every child has that potential.

Johnson began a successful detracking initiative in 1995 by requiring all 8th graders to take Algebra I. His aim was to provide rigorous academic courses for all students. Carefully studying the profiles of specific students in the district, he was able to pinpoint patterns of course-taking that opened doors to academic opportunity for some students and closed those doors for others. He made his case to faculty and parents, finding predictable resistance in both camps. Math teachers themselves were among the most vocal naysayers. One teacher quoted in the *Education Week* piece recalls that she and her fellow math teachers thought the change would be hard and didn't like the fact that they would no longer have math classes composed solely of advanced math students. Parents of those students likewise argued that their children would no longer have the opportunity to work with academic peers and that their achievement would suffer as a result. To the parents, Johnson continued to make his case clearly, persistently, and patiently. With the teachers who resisted the change, he listened carefully to understand their concerns and provided whatever support they needed to be successful in their new roles.

One of the early teacher detractors, now an advocate of detracking, explained in *Education Week* that Johnson is someone who is always supportive of teachers and the needs of teachers, always seeking their input. Another notes that Johnson works to know teachers as individuals, understand their various strengths, and capitalize on those unique strengths in order to maximize teachers' abilities in the classroom: "He doesn't get in the way. He knows how to get talent. He knows how to support talent" (Ujifusa, 2015, para. 23). Another colleague reflected that Johnson always has clear and careful plans mapped out to reach goals. "He's never going to come to us and say, 'Let's just do this and see how it goes.' The support [is] put in place to make [the plan] very successful" (Ujifusa, 2015, para. 8).

The *Education Week* profile goes on to describe how Johnson carefully evaluates the results of change to ensure that outcomes are positive. In the case of the switch to Algebra I for all 8th graders, his data are convincing. In 2014, the school system achieved a 97 percent pass rate on the state test. When Johnson finds a misstep in the direction he has asked others to take, he's not afraid to admit it: "You have to be able to say, 'I made a mistake,' and go back and relearn what you thought you knew well some time in the past" (Ujifusa, 2015, para. 28).

It has now been many years since Johnson eliminated the five-track system that once existed in Rockville Centre by working with teachers to ensure that students had the support they needed to succeed in more rigorous classes. "Once you separate [students] and put them in different places," he says in the *Education Week* piece, "they begin to think of themselves as something different" (Ujifusa, 2015, para. 27). Since 2011, all high school students in the district have taken International Baccalaureate coursework.

Johnson appears to be a leader who works from a vision that has driven his thinking and decision making for over 25 years. He is steady in the face of difficulty and persistent over time. He is consistently attuned to those whose efforts are essential to turning the vision into reality, hearing their concerns openly and using a broad range of mechanisms to address the concerns so he can ensure teachers' success. He is a careful planner who leaves little to chance or to the imagination, reassuring colleagues that there is a way ahead. He assesses regularly to understand outcomes and to inform his leadership of next steps. He is humble and never afraid to admit and learn from an error. He clearly works with a growth mindset toward both teachers and students—convinced that all people have the seeds of greatness in them and that the job of schools is to see to the development of that greatness in both the people who work there and the students who attend. We hope you see that these are the attributes we have commended and described in this book.

Dig Deep: In what ways does William H. Johnson's leadership represent key principles and practices from this book? In what ways do you see yourself consistently representing and enacting these same principles and practices of effective leadership for change? In what ways does the brief description of Johnson's work suggest areas for continuing growth and development in your leadership?

A Look Back and Ahead

We have tried to share with you our best knowledge—and that of many others—about the process of making a significant and positive change in schools to benefit young people and adults alike. There is no recipe for change, but there are guiding principles that have been tested and validated. There is no guarantee of easy success. But then worthwhile things are seldom easy. The figure on the facing page reviews the elements employed by leaders of successful moves to schoolwide differentiation. We have spent the majority of this book developing each of these elements. Although they do not always follow a completely "stepwise" sequence, they are always present, always interacting, and always in need of a leader's attention. We have encouraged you to explore and use each as you lead differentiation to deep institutionalization or permanence. We trust the principles are becoming clearer and more familiar to you, and we hope that you will find them valuable in investing your efforts to make significant and sustainable change on behalf of all children where you work.

We have another hope as well. On a recent National Public Radio show, a guest explained a particular technique playwrights often use to hook their audiences. They draw people into their plays by "breaking a ritual" or custom and letting the characters wrestle with the conflict that it produces. In the world of theater, seeing characters or events in ways we're *not* used to seeing them creates an edge that forms memories for the audience. Thus, in the theater, breaking the ritual is a good thing because it wakes us up in ways that produce the intended result—drama and memories.

We'd like to flip the metaphor and express our hope that all of us, as school leaders, will break the ritual more often to reduce the drama that our teachers and other colleagues too often feel.

The ritual in school improvement usually involves several predictable and, ultimately, failed steps. Across the country and beyond, as new innovations are introduced, we (1) spend lots of money on initial training and create lots of energy and conversation about the change, (2) launch the change before enough time has elapsed to create the culture to accept it, (3) expect practitioners to implement the change quickly and at deep levels, (4) assess student performance way too early in the change process without looking at changes in the adults first, and (5) abandon the change when the going gets tough and people begin to have trouble with the management of the change.

This is the "ritual" we see time and time again, played out in large and small contexts, and it creates unintended and unhealthy drama for teachers, leaders, parents, and ultimately, students. It also creates infertile ground that yields few results and inspires less and less confidence from all who view it. Rather than drawing people into important work, it alienates people from the change, creating a crisis of confidence and

LEADING for DIFFERENTIATION

Assess growth toward the vision of differentiation

Conduct rich conversations to maintain focus and momentum on differentiation

Predict and handle resistance to the change

Use collaborative, job-embedded professional development to support teacher understanding of differentiation

Understand and support adult learning and development throughout the life span of the change

Create an operational vision for differentiation and yearly change plans to make it happen

Make the commitment to change to differentiation

infecting them with the feeling that because the ritual is so predictable, *all* change efforts will result in next to nothing.

Despite firsthand experience with the husk of abandoned change efforts in schools, we remain optimistic because of the positive changes we have seen in schools led and managed by leaders who attend to both relationships and results. They operate with the simple idea that it is impossible to remove people from the technical aspects of change. They work from a meaningful vision, learn to communicate that vision compellingly, create teams of thinkers and planners to work with them, understand that change is difficult and will be earmarked by tension, know how to deal with tensions in productive ways, support the efforts they ask of colleagues so their colleagues become more successful as a result of their efforts, monitor progress—and *persist*. It is wise and informed persistence that leads to permanence. Paradoxically, permanence, to date, has a fleeting place in the landscape of educational change.

A recent research article (Dack, van Hover, & Hicks, 2015) serves as another piece of evidence in the argument for informed, focused, and persistent leadership for change in our schools. The article reports findings from a study looking at ways in which social studies teachers in grades 3–12 used "experiential instructional strategies" in their classes. This category of strategies includes things like simulations, enactments, and role-plays—approaches that move students away from primarily absorbing information and toward greater involvement in events and ideas that can help them make sense of what they are learning. Experiential strategies actively engage students in becoming part of history and should result in more active learning, more meaning making, and deeper thought than is typical with more teacher- and fact-focused approaches to learning.

In this study, researchers examined 438 videotaped lessons from 42 social studies teachers in 16 school districts, captured over a period of 4 years. The 42 teachers *volunteered* to have their lessons taped, which suggests that they felt at least relatively confident about their pedagogy. Researchers watched each lesson four times, coding the lessons according to criteria rooted in the literature of social studies education. In the end, only 14 of the 438 lessons used experiential approaches. Twelve of these 14 lacked a clear instructional purpose or were so inflexible in approach that student thinking was curtailed or the outcome was a significant misunderstanding of the content. Of the two lessons that did not demonstrate these problems, one used an experiential strategy solely for the purpose of recall of facts. In other words, teachers from this relatively large sample who likely felt their teaching was strong enough to be observed, taped, and analyzed failed almost totally to use approaches to teaching social studies that move students toward deeper involvement and understanding.

The article is noteworthy not because its findings are unusual but rather because it is so representative of the landscape of education. There is no shortage of approaches to teaching and learning that are genuinely promising in terms of student engagement, understanding, and achievement. And there are always some teachers who aspire to include those approaches in their work with students. In the absence of sustained and wise leadership, however, even the solid intentions of teachers who have the will to grow are often stillborn in the face of classroom complexity and the myriad pressures of teaching.

We believe that no significant and lasting change happens in schools without leaders who deeply understand, fully value, and determinedly cultivate real leadership for instructional change. Much of this book has been on the "how" to lead differentiation, and our desire is that you will not only use the frameworks, tools, and concepts in this book but will also create your own mechanisms for leading the work. To embed differentiation into daily effective practice requires grit, vision, and a devotion to the journey. Our students depend on us to consistently demonstrate characteristics so that they can acquire what they need to lead *us* into the future. We hope that you, as a reader of this book, will draw from it both the inspiration and the understanding to lead for schools that open the way to equity of access to excellence for all young people whose lives, for better or worse, will be molded by the decisions we make and how we breathe life into those decisions. In the end, we are hopeful that our efforts will contribute to growing school leaders committed to growing teachers who, in turn, will be more competent and confident in growing each learner in their care.

References

Beckhard, R., & Harris, R. (1987). *Organizational transitions: Managing complex change* (2nd ed.). Upper Saddle River, NJ: Pearson.

Berger, W. (2014). *A more beautiful question*. New York: Bloomsbury, USA.

Bui, S., Craig, S., & Imberman, S. (2012). Poor results for high achievers. *Education Next, 12*(1). Retrieved from http://educationnext.org/poor-results-for-high-achievers/

Burris, C., & Garrity, D. (2008). *Detracking for excellence and equity*. Alexandria, VA: ASCD.

Centers for Disease Control and Prevention. (2013). *Children's mental health—New report.* Retrieved from http://www.cdc.gov/features/childrensmentalhealth/

Cheliotes, L., & Reilly, M. (2010). *Coaching conversations: Transforming your school one conversation at a time*. Thousand Oaks, CA: Corwin.

Dack, H., van Hover, S., & Hicks, D. (2015). "Try not to giggle if you can help it": The implementation of experiential instructional techniques in social studies classrooms. *Journal of Social Studies Research, 39*(3). Available: http://www.sciencedirect.com/science/article/pii/S0885985X15000078

Danielson, C. (2009). *Talk about teaching*. Thousand Oaks, CA: Corwin Press.

Danielson, C. (2013). *Framework for Teaching Evaluation Instrument*. Retrieved from https://danielsongroup.org/framework/

Deal, T., & Peterson, K. (2000). *The leadership paradox: Balancing logic and artistry in schools*. San Francisco: Jossey-Bass.

Deci, E., & Flaste, R. (1996). *Why we do what we do: Understanding self-motivation*. New York: Penguin Books.

DuFour, R., DuFour, R., & Eaker, R. (2008). *Revisiting professional learning communities at work: New insights for improving schools*. Bloomington, IN: Solution Tree.

Dweck, C. (2006). *Mindset: The new psychology of success*. New York: Ballantine Books.

Earl, L. (2003). *Assessment as learning: Using classroom assessment to maximize student learning*. Thousand Oaks, CA: Corwin.

Education Week. (2015, February 24). *Leaders of 2015. Education Week's Leaders to Learn From*. Retrieved from http://leaders.edweek.org/leaders/2015/

Ellis, D. (2009). *How to hug a porcupine*. New York: Hatherleigh Press.

Evans, R. (2001). *The human side of school change: Reform, resistance, and the real-life problems of innovation*. San Francisco: Jossey-Bass.

Fullan, M. (2001a). *Leading in a culture of change*. San Francisco: Jossey-Bass.

Fullan, M. (2001b). *The new meaning of educational change* (3rd ed.). New York: Teachers College Press.

Fullan, M. (2007). *The new meaning of educational change* (4th ed.). New York: Teachers College Press.

Gallaher, R. (2005). The Change Formula. *Congregational Development*. Retrieved from http://www.congregationaldevelopment.com/storage/Change%20formula.pdf

Gamoran, A. (1992, October). Synthesis of research: Is ability grouping equitable? *Educational Leadership, 50*(2), 11–17.

Gamoran, A., Nystrand, M., Berends, M., & LePore, P. (1995). An organizational analysis of the effects of ability grouping. *American Educational Research Journal, 32*(4), 687–715.

Guskey, T. (2000). *Evaluating professional development*. Thousand Oaks, CA: Corwin.

Haberman, M. (1991). The pedagogy of poverty vs. good teaching. *Phi Delta Kappan, 73*(4), 290–294.

Hall, G. (1999). Using constructs and techniques from research to facilitate and assess implementation of an innovative mathematics program. *Journal of Classroom Interaction, 34*(1), 1–8.

Hall, G., & Hord, S. (2001). *Implementing change: Patterns, principles, and potholes*. Boston: Allyn and Bacon.

Hargreaves, A., & Fullan, M. (2012). *Professional capital: Transforming teaching in every school*. New York: Teachers College Press.

Hattie, J. (2009). *Visible learning: A synthesis of over 800 meta-analyses relating to achievement*. New York: Routledge.

Hattie, J. (2012). *Visible learning for teachers: Maximizing impact on learning*. New York: Routledge.

Hirsh, S., & Killion, J. (2007). *The learning educator: A new era for professional learning*. Oxford, OH: Learning Forward.

Hodges, H. (2001). Overcoming a pedagogy of poverty. In R. Cole (Ed.), *More strategies for educating everybody's children* (pp. 1–9). Alexandria, VA: ASCD.

Hord, S., & Roussin, J. (2013). *Implementing change through learning: Concerns-based concepts, tools, and strategies for guiding change*. Thousand Oaks, CA: Corwin.

Huberman, A., & Miles, M. (1984). *Innovation up close: How school improvement works*. New York: Plenum Press.

Joyce, B., & Calhoun, E. (2010). *Models of professional development: A celebration of educators*. Thousand Oaks, CA: Corwin.

Kegan, R., & Lahey, L. (2009). *Immunity to change: How to overcome it and unlock the potential in yourself and your organization*. Boston: Harvard Business School Press.

Kirkpatrick, D. (1959). Techniques for evaluating training programs. *Training and Development Journal, 13*(11).

Knight, J. (2011). *Unmistakable impact: A partnership approach for dramatically improving instruction*. Thousand Oaks, CA: Corwin.

Kohlberg, L. (1981). *The philosophy of moral development: Moral stages and the ideas of justice*. New York: Harper & Row.

Krogstad, J. M., & Fry, R. (2014, August 18). Dept. of Ed.'s projects public schools will be "majority-minority" this fall. *Fact-Tank: News in the Numbers*. Retrieved from http://www.pewresearch.org/fact-tank/2014/08/18/u-s-public-schools-expected-to-be-majority-minority-starting-this-fall/

Lawrence, P. (1969, January). How to deal with resistance to change. *Harvard Business Review*. Retrieved from https://hbr.org/1969/01/how-to-deal-with-resistance-to-change

Learning Forward. (2011). *Standards for professional learning*. Oxford, OH: Learning Forward.

Lewin, R., & Regine, B. (1999). *The soul at work: Unleashing the power of complexity science for business success.* London: Orion Business.

Little, J. (2008). Declaration of interdependence. *Journal of Staff Development, 29*(3), 53–56.

Marsh, H., Tautwein, U., Ludtke, O., Baumert, J., & Koller, O. (2007). The big-fish-little-pond effect: Persistent negative effects of selective high schools on self-concept after graduation. *American Educational Research Journal, 44*(3), 631–669.

Marzano, R., Waters, J., & McNulty, B. (2005). *School leadership that works: From research to results.* Alexandria, VA: ASCD.

Murphy, D. (2010). *You can't just say it louder: Differentiated strategies for comprehending nonfiction.* Huntington Beach, CA: Shell Education.

Murphy, M. (2014). *Orchestrating school change: Transforming your leadership.* Huntington Beach, CA: Shell Education.

National Center for Children in Poverty. (2014). *Child poverty.* Retrieved from http://www.nccp.org/topics/childpoverty.html

National Center for Education Statistics. (2013). *Characteristics of public and private elementary and secondary schools in the United States.* Washington, DC: U.S. Department of Education. Retrieved from http://nces.ed.gov/pubs2013/2013312.pdf

National Center for Education Statistics. (2014). *The condition of schools: English language learners.* Washington, DC: U.S. Department of Education. Retrieved from http://nces.ed.gov/programs/coe/indicator_cgf.asp

National Center for Learning Disabilities. (2014). *The state of learning disabilities* (3rd ed.). New York: Author.

National Research Council. (2000). *How people learn: Brain, mind, experience, and school.* Washington, DC: National Academy Press.

Oakes, J. (1985). *Keeping track: How schools structure inequality.* New Haven, CT: Yale University Press.

Patterson, K., Grenny, J., Maxfield, D., McMillan, R., & Switzler, A. (2013). *Crucial accountability: Tools for resolving violated expectations, broken commitments, and bad behavior* (2nd ed.). New York: McGraw-Hill.

Pearson, D., & Gallagher, M. (1983). The gradual release of responsibility model of instruction. *Contemporary Educational Psychology, 8,* 112–113.

Piaget, J. (1997). *The moral development of the child.* New York: Simon & Schuster.

Pink, D. (2009). *Drive: The surprising truth about what motivates us.* New York: Riverhead Books.

Powell, W., & Kusuma-Powell, O. (2015, May). Overcoming resistance to new ideas. *Phi Delta Kappan, 96*(8), 66–69.

Preckel, F., Gotz, T., & Frenzel, A. (2010). Ability grouping of gifted students: Effects on academic self-concept and boredom. *British Journal of Educational Psychology, 80*(3), 451–472.

Seaton, M., Marsh, H., & Craven, R. (2009). Big-fish-little-pond effect: Generalizability and moderation—Two sides of the same coin. *American Education Research Journal, 47*(2), 390–433.

Senge, P. (1999). *The dance of change: The challenges of sustaining momentum in learning organizations.* New York: Doubleday.

Sergiovanni, T. (1992). *Moral leadership: Getting to the heart of school improvement.* San Francisco: Jossey-Bass.

Shapiro, A. (2011, August 10). Learning with our friends: The zone of proximal development [blog post]. *Psychology Today.* Retrieved from https://www.psychologytoday.com/blog/healing-possibility/201108/learning-our-friends-the-zone-proximal-development

Sharratt, L., & Fullan, M. (2012). *Putting faces on the data.* Thousand Oaks, CA: Corwin.

Slavin, R. (1987). Ability grouping and achievement in the elementary school: A best evidence synthesis. *Review of Educational Research, 57,* 293–336.

Slavin, R. (1993). Ability grouping in the middle grades: Achievement effects and alternatives. *Elementary School Journal, 93,* 535–552.

Steenhuysen, J. (2013, March 20). U.S. autism estimates climb to 1 in 50 school-age children. *Reuters.* Retrieved from http://www.reuters.com/article/2013/03/21/us-usa-autism-idUSBRE92K00C20130321

Stone, D., Deci, E., & Ryan, R. (2009). Beyond talk: Creating autonomous motivation through self-determination theory. Retrieved from http://www.selfdetermination theory.org/SDT/documents/2009_StoneDeciRyan_JGM.pdf

Subban, P. (2006). Differentiated instruction: A research basis. *International Education Journal, 7*(7), 935–947.

Tennessee Department of Education. (2013). TEAM update, March 5, 2013. Retrieved from http://team-tn.org

Texas Leadership Center. (2014, June 23–24). Learning Forward Texas Leadership Development Process Training. Grapevine, Texas.

Tomlinson, C., Brighton, C., Hertberg, H., Callahan, C., Moon, T., Brimijoin, K., Conover, L. A., & Reynolds, T. (2003). Differentiating instruction in response to student readiness, interest, and learning profile in academically diverse classrooms: A review of literature. *Journal for the Education of the Gifted, 27*(2–3), 119–145.

Tomlinson, C., Brimijoin, K., & Narvaez, L. (2008). *The differentiated school: Making revolutionary changes in teaching and learning.* Alexandria, VA: ASCD.

Tomlinson, C., & Imbeau, M. (2013). Differentiated instruction: An integration of theory and practice. In B. Irby, G. Brown, R. Lara-Alecio, & S. Jackson (Eds.), *The handbook of educational theories for theoretical frameworks* (pp. 1097–1117). Charlotte, NC: Information Age.

Tomlinson, C., & McTighe, J. (2006). *Integrating differentiated instruction and Understanding by Design: Connecting content and kids.* Alexandria, VA: ASCD.

Tschannen-Moran, M. (2004). *Trust matters: Leadership for successful schools.* San Francisco: Jossey-Bass.

Tschannen-Moran, M., & Tschannen-Moran, B. (2010). *Evocative coaching: Transforming schools one conversation at a time.* San Francisco: Jossey-Bass.

Ujifusa, A. (2015, February 24). William H. Johnson: High expectations and access to rigor define a N.Y. educator's career. *Education Week Leaders to Learn From.* Retrieved from http://leaders.edweek.org/profile/william-h-johnson-superintendent-academic-detracking/

Uro, G., & Barrio, A. (2013). *English language learners in America's Great City Schools: Demographics, achievement, and staffing.* Washington, DC: Council of the Great City Schools. Retrieved from http://files.eric.ed.gov/fulltext/ED543305.pdf

Van Manen, M. (1986). *The tact of teaching.* New York: Scholastic.

Vygotsky, L. (1980). *Mind in society: The development of higher psychological processes.* Boston: Harvard University Press.

Vygotsky, L. (1986). *Thought and language* (2nd ed.). Boston: The MIT Press.

Walsh, J., & Sattes, B. (2010). *Leading through quality questioning: Creating capacity, commitment, and community.* Thousand Oaks, CA: Corwin.

Watanabe, M. (2008). Tracking in the era of high-stakes state accountability reform: Case studies of classroom instruction in North Carolina. *Teachers College Record, 110*(3), 489–534.

Waters, J., Marzano, R., & McNulty, B. (2003). *Balanced leadership: What 30 years of research tells us about the effect of leadership on student achievement.* Aurora, CO: Mid-continent Research for Education and Learning.

Wiggins, G., & McTighe, J. (2005). *Understanding by Design* (2nd ed.). Alexandria, VA: ASCD.

Wilhelm, J. (2001). *Improving comprehension with think-aloud strategies: Modeling what good readers do.* New York: Scholastic.

Index

Note: Page numbers followed by an italicized *f* indicate information contained in figures.

ability grouping, 11–12
achievement, student, 6–10
action research professional development, 78*f*
advanced learners, 4
analyzing student work, 77*f*
assessment, of differentiation implementation. *See* evaluation, of differentiation implementation
assessment-centered classrooms, 6, 96, 98*f*
autonomy motivational factor, 24–25, 25*f*, 48*f*, 72
awareness concerns, 82*f*

Bennett, Eve (case study), 83–84, 116–117
book studies, 78*f*
Bowertown Middle School case study, 66–67, 71
Brooks, James (case study), 92–93, 129–130

case analyses professional development, 78*f*
case studies
 Bennett, Eve, 83–84, 116–117
 Bowertown Middle School, 66–67, 71
 Brooks, James, 92–93, 129–130

case studies—(*continued*)
 Culver Middle School, 36–38
 Greeneville City Schools, 58–62, 60*f*, 61*f*
 Mountain View Intermediate School, 62–63
 Mountview Middle School, 131–132
 Northside Elementary School, 92–93, 129–130
 Peretti, Melinda, 92–93
 Reynolds, Bill, 140
 Simpson, Veronica, 21–22
 Walker, Vivian, 110
 Wallace County School District, 135–136
change formula, 139–140
change initiatives, phases of, 28–38, 32*f*, 36*f*, 80–85, 82*f*. *See also* implementation, of differentiation
change motivation. *See* motivation, for change
change resistance, 130–132
clarity, 141
classroom management, 7–8, 96, 99*f*
classrooms, traits of effective, 5–10
coaching professional development, 78*f*
cognitive development differences, 8
collaborative and facilitative leadership style, 100–102, 100*f*

collaborative and inviting leadership style, 100–102, 100f
command leadership style, 100–102, 100f
communication, 28–29
community-centered classrooms, 6
complexity, 141
consultative and participative leadership style, 100–102, 100f
conversations, leader–teacher. See leader–teacher conversations
Council of Chief State School Officers, vii
courses, 77f
Covey, Steven, 10
Crucial Accountability (Patterson et al.), 22, 134
cultural diversity, 4
Culver Middle School case study, 36–38
curriculum, 95–96, 98f
curriculum development and implementation, 77f

Danielson, Charlotte, vii
Deci, Edward, 23
demographic case for differentiation, 3–5
detracking, 147–149
differentiated instruction
    acceptance and recognition of, vii
    benefits of, 1–2
    demographic case for, 3–5
    ethical case for, 10–13
    Hattie on, 8–9
    permanence, 150f
    rationales for, 3–13
    research-based case for, 5–10
    what it is, and what it is not, 51f
The Differentiated School: Making Revolutionary Changes in Teaching and Learning (Tomlinson et al.), viii, 2–3
diversity and differentiation, 3–5, 11
Drive (Pink), 23
Dweck, Carol, 27

Earl, Lorna, 10–11
emotional issues, 4
English as a second language students, 3–5
ethical case for differentiation, 10–13
ethnic diversity, 4
evaluation, of differentiation implementation
    about, 109–112
    classroom observations, 119–120

evaluation, of differentiation—(continued)
    checklist for cultivating leadership competencies, 126
    Guskey's Levels of Evaluation for Professional Development, 113–114, 114f
    four critical questions, 124–125
    Novice-to-Expert Rubric for Differentiation, 120, 122–123
    one-legged interviews, 115
    scrapbook of evidence (impact), 125
    strategies for implementation phase, 117–122, 123f
    strategies for initiation phase, 115–117, 118f
    strategies for institutionalization phase, 122–124
    student outcomes, 121
    targets and rationale, 111–112, 111–114, 114f
experiential instructional strategies, 152

facilitation. See leader–teacher conversations; leading for differentiation
fixed mindset, 27, 133–134, 134f
Flaste, Richard, 23
formative assessment
    in evaluation of differentiation implementation, 110–111
    focus on, 6
    importance of, 8
Framework for Teaching Evaluation Instrument (Danielson), vii

gap conversations, 142–143
Georgia Teacher Keys Effectiveness System, vii
gradual release of responsibility framework, 73–79, 74f, 135–136
Greeneville City Schools case study, 58–62, 60f, 61f
group instruction, 9
growth mindset, 27, 72
Guskey, Tom, 113–114, 114f

Hall, Gene, 112
Hattie, John, 5, 6–9
heterogeneous grouping, 12
homogenous grouping, 12, 146
Hord, Shirley, 112
How People Learn (National Research Council), 5–6

"How to Deal with Resistance to Change" (Lawrence), 127, 130
How to Hug a Porcupine (Ellis), 127–128

immersion professional development, 77*f*
impact concerns, 81, 82*f*
implementation, of differentiation
    change motivation during, 28–35, 32*f*
    change motivation factors, 23–27, 25*f*, 26*f*
    change resistance (*See* resistance to differentiation implementation)
    chief professional developer's role, 13
    effects of, 13–14
    evaluation of (*See* evaluation, of differentiation implementation)
    implementation dip, 36*f*, 57*f*, 128–129
    implementation phase, 30–33, 32*f*, 117–122, 123*f*
    initiation phase, 28–30, 84, 115–117, 118*f*
    institutionalization phase, 33–35, 122–124
    key learning targets, 15*f*
    leader–teacher conversations (*See* leader–teacher conversations)
    leading (*See* leading for differentiation)
    mindset, vii–viii, 27
    phases of, and motivation, 28–38, 32*f*, 36*f*
    readiness for, 39–41, 40*f*
    teacher stages of concern, 80–85, 82*f*
implementation phase of implementation effort, 30–33, 32*f*, 117–122, 123*f*
initiation phase of implementation effort, 28–30, 84, 115–117, 118*f*
institutionalization phase of implementation effort, 33–35, 122–124
instruction, 96, 99*f*
intentionality, 7
interdependence, 69
intrinsic motivation, 22–23
invitational learning environments, 7

job-embedded professional development, 68–69, 68*f*
Johnson, William H., 147–149

Knight, Jim, 105
knowledge-centered classrooms, 6
KUDs, 13–15, 15*f*, 111

labeling, 7, 12
leader–teacher conversations. *See also* leading for differentiation
    about, 88–90
    characteristics of productive, 90–94, 91*f*
    checklist for cultivating leadership competencies, 108
    choosing topics for, 94
    critical elements to discuss, 95–98, 98*f*–99*f*
    effective methods for, 99–102, 100*f*
    gap conversations, 142–143
    layered approach to, 91–92, 91*f*
    Leadership Preference Continuum, 100*f*
    listening skills, 105–107, 106*f*
    Novice-to-Expert rubric, 98*f*–99*f*
    planning guidelines, 103–105
    questioning process, 102–105
    skills required for, 105–107, 106*f*
leading for differentiation. *See also* leader–teacher conversations
    change motivation factors, 23–27, 25*f*, 26*f*
    change motivation inhibitors, 21–23
    checklist for cultivating leadership competencies, 42
    change resistance (*See* resistance to differentiation implementation)
    chief professional developer's role, 13–15, 39–41
    components of, 151*f*
context of initiatives, 2–3
    during implementation phase, 30–33
    during initiation phase, 28–30
    during institutionalization phase, 33–35
    KUDs, 13–15, 15*f*
    leadership styles, 99–102, 100*f*
    teachers as change targets, 19–21
    traits needed, 17–18
    vision and, 45–48, 48*f*
Leaning Forward, 69, 70*f*, 84, 100
learning communities, 70*f*
learning differences, 8
learning disabilities, 4
learning environments, 7, 95, 98*f*
limited English proficiency students, 3–5
listening skills, 105–107, 106*f*, 143

mastery motivational factor, 26–27, 48*f*, 72
mental health issues, 4

mentoring professional development, 78*f*
mindful listening, 105–107, 106*f*
Mindset (Dweck), 27
moral development, 10–13
moral leadership, 16
motivation, for change
    autonomy, 24–25, 25*f, 48f*
    factors that enhance, 23–27, 25*f, 26f*
    factors that impede, 21–23
    implementation dip, 36*f*
    during implementation phases, 28–38,
      32*f,* 36*f*
    intrinsic motivation, 22–23
    mastery, 26–27, 48*f*
    operational vision and, 48*f*
    professional development and, 72
    purpose, 25–26, 26*f,* 48*f*
motivation, student, 8
Mountain View Intermediate School case
    study, 62–63
Mountview Middle School case study,
    131–132

National Association for the Education of
    Young Children, vii
National Association of Elementary School
    Principals, vii
National Association of Secondary School
    Principals, vii
National Board of Professional Teaching
    Standards, vii
National Middle School Association, vii
need, 141
New York Approved Teacher Practice
    Rubrics, vii
Northside Elementary School case study,
    92–93, 129–130
Novice-to Expert Continuum for teachers'
    differentiation development, 15, 16*f*
Novice-to-Expert Rubric for
    Differentiation, viii, 98*f*–99*f,* 120, 122–123

one-legged interviews, 115, 119, 128
operational vision
    about, 44–45, 45*f*
    examples of statements, 54–55
    checklist for cultivating leadership
      competencies, 64
    and individual motivation, 48*f*
    power of, 48, 49*f*
    preparing school staff for, 48–50
    process for crafting, 50–55, 52*f*–53*f*
    purpose of, 45–48

operational vision—(*continued*)
    and yearly change plans, 55–58, 96
optimism, 7

pedagogy of plenty, 11–12
pedagogy of poverty, 11
Peretti, Melinda (case study), 92–93
phases of change initiatives, 28–38, 32*f,*
    36*f,* 80–85, 82*f. See also* implementation,
    of differentiation
Pink, Daniel H., 23
planning, school, common process for,
    43–44
poverty, 4
practicality, 142
professional development
    about, 65
    adaptation over time, 66–68
    checklist for cultivating leadership
      competencies, 86
    developing mastery through, 72–76,
      74*f*
    differentiated, 66, 84
    effective designs for, 76–80, 77*f*–78*f*
    evaluation of (*See* evaluation, of
      differentiation implementation)
    and gradual release of responsibility
      framework, 73–76, 74*f*
    Guskey's Levels of Evaluation for
      Professional Development, 113–114,
      114*f*
    job-embedded and interdependent,
      68–69, 68*f*
    as key change element for
      differentiation, 65–76
    standards-basis for, 69–72, 70*f*
    teacher concerns about, 80–85, 82*f*
    and visioning process, 50, 51*f*
    and zone of proximal development,
      72–73, 75
purpose motivational factor, 25–26, 26*f,*
    47–48, 47*f,* 72

quality, 142
questioning process, leadership, 102–105

readiness chart, 40*f*
relationships, 20
research-based case for differentiation,
    5–10
resistance to differentiation
    implementation
      about, 127–128, 144

resistance to differentiation
implementation—(*continued*)
change formula, 139–140
change resistance generally, 130–132
checklist for cultivating leadership
competencies, 145
factors affecting teacher buy-in,
141–142
gap conversations, 142–143
impatience and speed, 135–136
leader's potential contribution to,
133–134, 134*f*
likely timing of, 128–130
management guidelines for, 136–138,
138*f*
strategies to manage, 139–144
respectful environments, 7–8, 69, 143
Reynolds, Bill (case study), 140
Rockville Centre Union Free School
District, 147–149
Roussin, Jim, 112

school change, 19–21, 150–153
second-order change, vii–viii, 19
self concerns, 81, 82*f*
seminars, 77*f*
Simpson, Veronica (case study), 21–22
social aspects of change, 130–132
Stages of Concern, for change, 80–85, 82*f*,
115, 116
storytelling, 49
student-centered classrooms, 5, 11
student diversity, 3–5
student outcomes, 121
study groups, 78*f*, 79

task concerns, 81, 82*f*
teachers. *See also* professional
development
change motivation of (*See* motivation,
for change)
change resistance of (*See* resistance
to implementation)
competence and confidence of, 2
differentiation as expert instruction, 10
expertise of, 8
factors affecting teacher buy-in,
141–142
implementation effects, 13–14
as individual change targets, 20

teachers—(*continued*)
key learning targets, 15*f*
Stages of Concern, 80–85, 82*f*, 115, 116
student-centered, 7
technical aspects of change, 130–132
Tennessee Educator Acceleration Model
Teacher Evaluation Rubrics, vii
Title I services, 4
tracking, 11–12, 146–149
training, 77*f*, 79
trust, 7

unrelated concerns, 80–81

Villegas, Rene, 66–67, 71
Visible Learning (Hattie), 5, 6–9
Visible Learning for Teachers (Hattie), 5,
6–9
vision
about, 43
defined, 44, 45, 45*f*
linking with action, 28–29
and motivation, 35
operational vision, 44–45, 45*f*, 46–58,
52*f*–53*f*, 57*f*
yearly change plans, 44, 45, 45*f*, 56–63,
57*f*, 59*f*, 60*f*, 61*f*
Vygotsky, Lev, 72–73

Walker, Vivian (case study), 110
Wallace County School District case
study, 135–136
*Why We Do What We Do: Understanding
Self-Motivation* (Deci & Flaste), 23
worries, checking on, 50

yearly change plans
about, 44, 45, 45*f*, 56–58, 57*f*
elements to focus on, 96–97
Greeneville City Schools case study,
58–62, 60*f*, 61*f*
and leader–teacher conversations,
96–98
Mountain View Intermediate School
(case study), 62–63
operational vision and, 55–58
powerful effects of, 62–63
process for creating, 59*f*

zone of proximal development, 72–73, 75

About the Authors

Carol Ann Tomlinson began her career in education in the public school system, where she spent 21 years as a classroom teacher and in administrative roles. During that time, she taught high school, preschool, and middle school students in the content areas of English and language arts, history, and German. She also served as director of programs for advanced and struggling learners and as school community relations coordinator. While a teacher in the Fauquier County (Virginia) Public Schools, she received recognition as Outstanding Teacher at Warrenton Junior High School, Jaycees Outstanding Young Educator, American Legion Outstanding Educator, and Soroptimist Distinguished Women in Education. She was named Virginia's Teacher of the Year in 1974.

Carol is currently the William Clay Parrish Jr. Professor and Chair of Educational Leadership, Foundations, and Policy at the University of Virginia's Curry School of Education, where she is also co-director of the University's Institutes on Academic Diversity. She works with both graduate and undergraduate students, particularly in the areas of curriculum and differentiated instruction. She was named Outstanding Professor at Curry in 2004 and received an All-University Teaching Award in 2008. In 2015, Carol was named number 16 of the 200 higher education faculty members in the United States deemed most influential in terms of shaping dialogue about education by the *Education Week* Edu-Scholar Public Influence Rankings.

Carol is author of more than 250 books, book chapters, articles, and other educational materials including (for ASCD): *How to Differentiate Instruction in Mixed-Ability Classrooms*; *The Differentiated Classroom: Responding to the Needs of All Learners* (2nd edition); *Fulfilling the Promise of the Differentiated Classroom: Strategies and Tools for Responsive Teaching*; *Integrating Differentiated Instruction and Understanding by Design: Connecting Content and Kids* (with Jay McTighe); *The Differentiated School: Making Revolutionary Changes in Teaching and Learning* (with Kay Brimijoin and Lane Narvaez); and *Leading and Managing a Differentiated Classroom* (with Marcia Imbeau). Her ASCD books have been translated into 13 languages.

Carol works regularly throughout the United States and internationally with educators who seek to create classrooms that are more effective for academically diverse student populations. She can be reached at Curry School of Education, P.O. Box 400277, Charlottesville, VA 22904 or by e-mail at cat3y@virginia.edu or www.differentiationcentral.com.

Michael Murphy is a national educational coach, facilitator, and consultant currently living in Dallas, Texas. He draws from 39 years of educational experience in urban, suburban, and rural school district settings as he trains and works with teachers, teacher leaders, school leaders, and district leaders across North America. Much of Mike's work supports school and district leaders in planning and implementing large-scale improvement initiatives, visioning, understanding change and its effect on people, evaluating school improvement progress, designing exceptional professional development, and engaging people in productive, relationship-rich, results-based conversations. Since 2009, he has consulted with school leaders in 17 U.S. states and two Canadian provinces, and he has presented in numerous state, national, and international symposia and conferences.

Mike's personal public school experiences include his work as teacher, elementary specialist, assistant principal, principal, director of planning and evaluation, special assistant to the superintendent, assistant superintendent, and acting superintendent, all in Texas. He holds a bachelor of fine arts degree and a master's degree in elementary education from Texas Tech University and a doctorate in curriculum and instruction from the University of North Texas. He has published numerous articles for national journals and is a contributing author or lead author for four educational books. Mike has been a long-time guest presenter at the University of Virginia's Summer Institute on Academic Diversity; has trained several thousand principals, assistant principals, and central office staff during his relationship with the Tennessee Academy for School Leaders; and is the former director of programs for the National Staff Development Council (now Learning Forward). He can be reached at 1309 Melrose Drive, Richardson, TX 75080, or via e-mail at mmurphy170@gmail.com.

Related ASCD Resources

At the time of publication, the following ASCD resources were available (ASCD stock numbers appear in parentheses). For up-to-date information about ASCD resources, go to www.ascd.org. You can search the complete archives of *Educational Leadership* at http://www.ascd.org/el.

ASCD EDge Group

Exchange ideas and connect with other educators interested in topics like differentiated instruction, leadership in schools, change and school culture, and the Whole Child on the social networking site ASCD EDge™ at http://ascdedge.ascd.org/

Online Courses

Differentiated Instruction: Teaching with Student Differences in Mind (#PD11OC138)

Differentiated Instruction: The Curriculum Connection (#PD11OC116M)

Print Products

The Differentiated Classroom: Responding to the Needs of All Learners, 2nd edition by Carol Ann Tomlinson (#108029)

The Differentiated School: Making Revolutionary Changes in Teaching and Learning by Carol Ann Tomlinson, Kay Brimijoin, and Lane Narvaez (#105005)

Leading Change in Your School: How to Conquer Myths, Build Commitment, and Get Results by Douglas B. Reeves (#109019)

Professional Development for Differentiating Instruction: An ASCD Action Tool by Cindy A. Strickland (#109042)

"What Differentiation Is and Is Not" (Poster) (#115068)

Video

The Differentiated Classroom: Responding to the Needs of Elementary Learners (DVD) (#615047)

The Differentiated Classroom: Responding to the Needs of Secondary Learners (DVD) (#615048)

The Differentiated School: Making Revolutionary Changes in Teaching and Learning (DVD) (#610008)

Leadership for Differentiating Instruction (DVD and Facilitator's Guide) (#607038)

A Visit to a School Moving Toward Differentiation (DVD with Viewer's Guide) (#607133)

THE WHOLE CHILD The Whole Child Initiative helps schools and communities create learning environments that allow students to be healthy, safe, engaged, supported, and challenged. To learn more about other books and resources that relate to the whole child, visit www.wholechildeducation.org.

For more information: send e-mail to member@ascd.org; call 1-800-933-2723 or 703-578-9600, press 2; send a fax to 703-575-5400; or write to Information Services, ASCD, 1703 N. Beauregard St., Alexandria, VA 22311-1714 USA.